Seasons of a Fly Fisher

Fly Fishing Canada's Western Waters

Brian Smith

SEASONS OF A FLY FISHER

Fly Fishing Canada's Western Waters

Brian Smith

CAITLIN PRESS

Photo pages 2–3: Sunset at Hobson Lake. Photo by Erich Franz. Pages 4–5: Roche Lake. Photo by Glenn Gerbrandt. Pages 6–7: Pelican Lake. Photo by Richard Barrie. Page 8: Sunset fades on Kildala Arm in Kitimat. Photo by Brian Smith. Page 10: Indian paintbrush. Photo by Glenn Gerbrandt.

To my fly-fishing "partners," whose fine company I have enjoyed immensely over my forty-five years of fly fishing: my wife, Lois, and our children, Kevin, Graham, BJ and Darcie; Grant Stevens, Donald Clarke, Daniel Erasmus, Kevin Beatty, Jim Lewis, Bob Graham and Dale Freschi. Each of you has enriched my life tenfold.

Contents

Introduction

We become fishers by introduction, and fly fishers by trial and elimination. If your journey to fly fishing resembled mine, you began with a whittled willow pole, string line, rusty old hook and freshly dug garden worm, then graduated to an inexpensive bait-casting rod and reel, and ended up a fly fisher with an astonishing array of equipment and tackle amassed over the years, which most of us could not possibly afford without winning the lottery.

My passion for fishing began innocently. My first memory of the sport was my father taking me and my older brother, Michael, when we were about four and five years old, to a small river in rural northern Alberta to try our luck at catching pickerel, which in the 1950s were grossly abundant in most of that area's streams, and probably still are today. I can see the picture in my mind, almost sixty years later—Mike and me standing on a bridge with Dad doing the fishing, him hooking and losing an enormous fish, which I can still visualize grabbing the bait and heading north upriver with a ferocious display of strength and determination. "Man!" I thought, "If I could catch one of those, Mom would be proud of me!"

There were a few more fishing expeditions in Alberta before we moved west to Surrey, BC, in 1953, one at Lesser Slave Lake where I recall my first boat ride and remember us bringing home a wooden icebox full of pickerel, and Mom and Dad getting the deep fryer going to cook a batch of those marvellous-tasting fish. On yet another occasion, I figured I was old enough (all of four years) to go fishing by myself, so I lined up my gear and took off—looking like Huckleberry Finn—to Lesser Slave Lake about a mile away with our dog, Bonzo. I got into a lot of trouble for doing it as I recall, and blaming Bonzo didn't cut me any slack either... heck, I just wanted to go fishing.

I have fished for as long as I can remember. My Irish/English relatives, the Kennys on Mom's side, were pioneer fur farmers in the Beaverlodge area of northern Alberta, settling land west of there in 1913. They ranched mink and silver fox, moving to Faust, Alberta, in the early 1930s. When the clan relocated to the BC Lower Mainland in the early 1950s, the Smiths followed along.

Fishing continued to play a huge part in my upbringing. Mike and I rode bikes to the Nicomekl and Serpentine rivers in South Surrey to fish for bullheads, and the odd trout. Success led us to expeditions on the Little Campbell River near the US border, where we learned to angle for cut-throat trout, steelhead and coho salmon.

But it was BC's Interior that beckoned me. My dad wasn't a fisher-man, nor was anyone else in the family, but like most dads he understood that you need to introduce your children to new experiences and from there they develop their own pursuits. When Mike and I were about thir-teen and twelve, respectively, Dad took us on a "boys-only" camping trip (minus our four sisters) into the dry belt of the Interior, where rainbow trout were the quarry. We fished Loon, Missezula and Harmon lakes on that trip and I distinctly remember catching my first Interior rainbow on hook and worm in the Bonaparte River, right under the Hwy 97 North Bridge in Cache Creek.

We enjoyed several more trips to the Interior during my formative years and I credit my dad—even though he wasn't a "real" fisherman—with start-ing me on the path of this fishing journey that I have followed all my life.

My fly-fishing pursuit began when I was fourteen years old, on a Boy Scout camping trip, while watching our assistant Scoutmaster (Akela) Hugo Peterson entice rainbow trout to a Royal Coachman dry fly in Davis Lake near Haney, BC. We fished from the shoreline and logjams where, unlike worm fishing, you could see trout come from the depths or the cover of logs to intercept the floating fly. They would slowly wiggle to the target, surround the imitation, and even more slowly back up to suck the fake insect into their mouths. Then there was the confusion and rush to perceived safety when the mistake was realized. Fifty years later, that picture still holds fascination for me!

Fly fishers come first to the fly rod, then to fly tying, and a few, like me, advance to rod building and writing about fly fishing. For some, it's a matter of cost control (flies are expensive); for others, it's a need to be creative and thoughtful, a joy of expression that is an art form. Fly tying begins with copying proven pattern samples, and progresses over many years to a very personal style and signature for your models. The accumulation of materials takes many decades of rooting through fly shops, bargain bins and garage sales, not to mention eyeing every barnyard chicken coop, mounted bird display and road-kill site as a possible source of inexpensive hackle or fur for your newest invention on the fly-tying vise.

It isn't fair that a fine collection of fly rods should come easily to a fly fisher. Rather, it should be a gathering of many years of searching, trading, bartering and testing before the reward of a well-used set of fly rods becomes a fixture in the palm of a seasoned fly fisher's hand. The fly-fishing world is ripe with new technology. Fly-rod designers and engineers make a good living blending glass and graphite fibres, inventing revolutionary tapers that fossilize every piece of equipment that came before it.

Nothing should be taken for granted when it comes to a good fly rod. It might take time and many outings to become comfortable with, but it isn't difficult to be infatuated with your choice right from the minute you acquire it, because the tool is judged by "feel" more than the price. Everything has to be right: colour, grip, reel seat, action, and even the tube and carrying case, to be called "one" of your collections. Call us fanatics, but we fly fishers know what we like, and are darned possessive about it.

Our favourite fishing places are everywhere—in our dreams, our desires, around every corner and bend, every path and in the backs of our lonely minds. You cannot possibly be a complete fly fisher without craving to try every spot on the earth that holds a trout, or at the very least a fish that will rise to a dry fly. Good cigars, a pleasant companion, a well-worn pair of boots and waders, your favourite fly rod and a fine piece of water to fish—what more could you possibly ask for in life?

In British Columbia, we live in what is likely the most geographically diverse piece of land in the world. Travelling the province south to north from Vancouver, it takes about twenty-four hours' driving time to reach the Yukon border. You begin your journey on the humid West Coast, the most temperate climate in Canada. In three hours, you penetrate desert country on the Interior Plateau, enter the sub-boreal forests of the Central Interior six hours later, traverse into the grain belt of the Peace Country several hours after crossing the Rocky Mountains, and still you are faced with a six-hour wilderness drive to meet the Yukon. Along this journey, you can angle for various species of saltwater and freshwater fish—five species of Pacific salmon, six types of trout, Rocky Mountain whitefish, grayling and several kinds of coarse fish. All varieties can be tackled with a fly rod; the fish can range in size from half a kilogram (kg) and smaller to 35 kg and larger.

The seasons of a fly fisher come and go; years quickly turn into decades and those to a life lived. Our pursuits are endless, our fishing thoughts and desires hopelessly engraved in our lonely souls; we pray that we'll have the health to continue the search next season. As we age, we reflect on the passing of this year's season and wonder if it might be our last. Is there really a spot in heaven for us after missing all those church services while wandering the countryside with fly rod in hand?

Our journey in this book takes us through the months of a typical year in a fly fisher's season and its productive fly patterns, while travelling into a variety of fishing places in British Columbia and Alberta that I have personally enjoyed and loved for their angling adventures. We'll begin in March, searching creeks and rivers for fishable water, and then chase April ice-off into the North Cariboo and Central Interior, slip into the Kootenays for a few weeks in summer and finally tackle the fall fly fishing of the Bulkley Valley and North Coast. We'll also touch on southern Alberta's fabulous cutthroat fishery, and the frisky rainbows of the world-famous Bow and Highwood rivers, places etched forever in my mind, where my boys and I spend a few weeks every summer rejoicing in our fly-fishing sport and making lifelong memories. Enjoy!

Brian Smith
May 30, 2012

March: Spring Awakens

When the first fair winds of March caress the BC Interior, our natural world awakens from winter's grasp. Animals stir from their dens, the earliest migratory birds begin to appear, insects hatch from shallow ponds to nourish arriving birdlife, lakes and rivers break from the long spell of ice-laden water and fly fishers look eagerly toward a fresh new year. For me, spring arrives when I hear my first robin singing from the tops of trees that are still caught in winter's clutch. Our local chickadees and tree sparrows have been regular visitors at the feeders all winter, even during frigid days of -30°C, joined by pileated and downy woodpeckers and the always-present mischievous grey squirrel family that keeps my wife, Lois, and I company through all seasons.

We've had enough of winter—it's time for the harmony of early spring: joyful sounds of mating songbird flocks that arrive daily, distant honking of Canada geese as they wing slowly northward to their breeding habitats and the ever-present chattering of ducks that visit open-water sewerage lagoons in the neighbourhood. For the strong, they have survived another year, and justly endured another long perilous journey to their summer breeding grounds in the north, a flight their ancestors have made for thousands of years.

Interior fly fishers welcome spring—it's a well-deserved reward for enduring another northern winter. We choose to live here, expecting no sympathy for doing so, although it's mighty tempting to hope for an early opening of the fishing season and the prize of an extra month of fishing time. It's happened several times during my twenty years in the north—those March early openings—but it completely alters the summer period. Insect hatches are about time and temperature. When spring comes too early, water warms more quickly, affecting greatly the prolonged summer bug emergences that we usually enjoy.

We don't have summer doldrums in our northern waters as they suffer in the Southern Interior lakes—you can always find a productive fishing zone up here. When the North Cariboo lakes sometimes turn off after a lingering summer hot spell, the rivers are then in prime fishing condition. If fishing lakes is your preference, you only need to venture farther north up Hwy 97 to continue fishing still waters along the Rocky Mountain Trench, places that never get enough hot weather to turn them off. For ·a fly fisher, this North Country abounds with prospects unequalled anywhere in the world.

All I can say about trying to fly fish the month of March in the north is that it's totally unpredictable. Around Prince George the lakes rarely open in March, but I do recall Tory Lake being half-open and producing lethargic, shocked trout one late March weekend in the early 1990s. In Quesnel, Dragon Lake will occasionally be ice-free by the last week of March or first week of April, but in most years ice-off normally happens during the second or third week of April.

During March, the best bet to wet a fly line and quench the rigours of cabin fever in the Prince George area is the little Crooked River. Other northern rivers exempt from spring closure are the Parsnip, Bowron, Nechako and Willow rivers, but they tend to be more ice-bound and treacherous than the Crooked during winter. I don't like to rule them out, but I concentrate on the Crooked.

Your next best option is to venture west and try for cutthroat and prime winter steelhead on the Kitimat River system. Steelhead from the summer-run of the Skeena system are still hanging around the Kalum, Copper and Lakelse rivers through winter months, but they are in spawning condition, and not nearly the challenge, nor do they possess the strength and vitality they presented to fly fishers the previous fall. We prefer to leave them be, let them conserve their strength for the spawn, and return to the sea where they will regain their once proud vigour and again return to their native rivers to reproduce.

Early spring fishing north of parallel 52 is predictable only by the current weather status, which can change from warm plus-Celsius figures one day to a drifting, blinding snowstorm overnight. Up here, a safe betting man doesn't carry fly-fishing gear on March road trips, but for me the chance to wet a line after a long winter is always too overwhelming to leave the equipment at home.

Crooked River

You're darned if you do, and more darned if you don't try your fishing luck in our Crooked River during early spring. After all, the Crooked is one of the few rivers open to fishing year-round in the north. Blessed by warm spring water seeping from Livingstone Springs and many others,

The chance to wet a line after a long winter is always too overwhelming to leave the equipment at home. Brian Smith photo.

the Crooked is a winter haven for whistling swans, their stark beauty and graceful aura blending peacefully into the snowbanks of the meadow-meandering Crooked.

Fishing the Crooked in March takes a bit of courage, and some careful manoeuvring through snowbanks, drifts, willow thickets and the many beaver dams that criss-cross the stream. Forget the pontoon boat in most places on the river during early spring; it's a walk-and-wade effort that will get you into the stream, and the easiest way to get around is to stay in the stream and wade, but you must locate the gravel sections to do so. The silt corners and soft bottom pieces of this little watercourse are death traps. You need to fish the Crooked with a buddy in early spring, someone to share your grief and rescue you when you perhaps make a wrong step and take a cold, unexpected dunking in frigid water.

Flowing north from Summit Lake and marking the transition from Pacific to Arctic watershed, lined by willows for most of its 100-km length, the Crooked is a wildlife watchers' paradise, but much of it is unproductive fishing water—you need to do some prospecting. Find the gravel beds, corners and slots that hold fish and you will be rewarded with stacks of wild native rainbow trout, fish that have common genetic links to the original northern species of the Carp Lake system, progeny that developed from receding glaciers ten thousand years ago. Along with natural rainbows, you'll also find Rocky Mountain whitefish that will rise to dry flies, suckers that will swallow your nymph patterns and the odd Dolly Varden or bull trout predator that will take any large streamer offering that looks like a meal.

The Crooked is only forty minutes north of the Hart Highlands residential area of Prince George. Although the banks are still snow-bound in March and will remain so until mid-April, there are many spots that are spring-fed with warm water from deep underground artesian sources that keep the flow going year-round. During March, trout and coarse fish that have wintered in lakes the Crooked flows out of, into or through (Summit, Davie, Kerry, Redrocky and McLeod) leave their winter survival habitat and return to the meandering Crooked. Mature trout will spawn, release their progeny and recover through a spring and summer season; immature fish will continue to develop while gorging on the prolific insect life of the stream.

Some of the best and most popular sections of the Crooked are high-lighted below. This little stream, however, is one of those rare gems. It beckons to fly fishers, inviting them to spend some time poking around to discover their own stretches of water and holes that are seldom fished. Once found, they will likely be yours for a long time if you keep them a secret. By releasing the trout, which is recommended for wild fish, you'll have your own aquarium whenever visiting "your" spot, albeit the fish will get a little larger and smarter every season.

Railroad Track

There are many glimpses of the river along Hwy 97 North, begin-ning with your first sight about 8 km from the outflow at Summit Lake, approximately 60 km from Prince George and 3 km past Log Lake Forest Service Road.

This spot is marked by a culvert, concrete barrier and short right turn-off to a parking area, but the best spot to park a vehicle is about half a kilo-metre farther north, where there's another short turn-in on the left near the railway tracks. Wader-up, clamber over the tracks with your 2- or 3-weight fly rod and a box of flies and you'll be looking at one of the nicest little pieces of corner water found anywhere in the river.

From this entry point, you can work your way upstream for quite a distance fishing gravel-lined pockets, searching for trout under and around sunken logs, drifting your offering on the edges of grass-lined slots and locating productive creek mouths and corners that pop up every time the river makes a short turn. It's easy to spend half a day in this pleasing little piece of water.

100 Road Bridge

The next section of the Crooked that is usually ice-free in March is the 100 Road Bridge area, accessed by turning west onto the 100 Road about 65 km north of Prince George, just 5 km past the railroad track section discussed above. This segment is only 3 km off the highway, has a small three-unit campsite for those who might enjoy winter camping along with their fly-fishing experience, and contains some of the nicest-looking water on the Crooked. The river upstream, downstream and through the middle of this gravel-marked part of the stream sports a variety of fish-holding habitat: a deep corner under the bridge, a soft run upstream, placid water just below the campsite and slot water pretty much everywhere throughout this spot. For the more adventurous, a hike upriver should be in order, for I've heard there is some really good water just around the next bend…

200 Road Bridge

Continuing up Hwy 97 North past the community of Bear Lake, 70 km north of Prince George, the next fishable section of the Crooked is accessed by turning west onto the Davie Muskeg (200) Forest Service Road, the first left turn past the Petrocan station in Bear Lake. About 5 km down this road, you'll come across the Crooked River Canyon Recreation Site, a small, forested three-unit campsite alongside the river that lends access to what is arguably the best section of water on the river. You can also access this stretch by continuing along 100 Road from the 100 Bridge campsites to the 213-km corner; turn right and continue 3 km to the bridge. All sections of the Crooked River above the 200 Bridge are exempt from spring closure; below the bridge it's closed April 1 to June 30.

Working the river upstream, this piece of water is best accessed by pontoon boat or canoe, which you can paddle upriver about thirty minutes from the road bridge, allowing you to fish the Livingstone Springs segment and some nice riffle water above the springs, and then slowly fish your way back downriver to your vehicle.

The most distant spot on this part of the stream features a pool and tail-out at the end of a quick, rocky run coming out of a forested segment. It is difficult to get a boat above this pool and the water is unproductive. It signals the beginning of the willow-lined meadow section that flows slowly downstream to the bridge. You will want to fish this and all downstream parts to the bridge thoroughly, because the trout move around and can be discovered almost anywhere along the return journey.

Livingstone Springs is not visibly marked, but recognizable by a swampy area of willows and grassy-looking weed cover about a twenty-minute paddle upstream from the 200 Bridge. The springs weep into the river from the willow thicket and trout lie in waiting to take advantage of augmented insect abundance and activity from the influx of warm, oxygenated water.

The area around the campsite, the corner upstream and the bend downstream from 200 Bridge are all productive spots for trout to congregate; as well, the run just above the bridge contains productive water that will harbour some nice trout through the winter season.

Winter Fly Patterns for the Crooked River

During winter, a fish's metabolism is much slower than in summer. It expends as little effort as possible to survive the worst time of year, a season when food and nutrients are scarce, water temperature is near freezing and oxygen levels are grossly depleted. Consider a trout in summertime that will charge across a pool for a spotted caddis slowly drifting along a riffle. That same fish during winter will be lying on the bottom looking down, waiting for a nymph to pass its window, or scrounging the bottom of the stream for cased caddis larvae—anything edible is the menu; survival its objective.

You must take a different approach to your fly-fishing sport in winter. For the majority of us who can't afford a winter vacation in the south on a regular basis, we must adapt our thinking to using nymph patterns, or suffer from dry-fly anxiety until June when major summer hatches will begin.

Although I personally cringe at the thought of using a strike indicator on my line, it is surely the best method for a slow, meandering stream like the little Crooked during winter. A sink-tip line set-up will gather more bottom debris than fish, especially on a quiet willow-infested river like this one. A floating line, weighted nymph system will get you the right drifts some of the time. However, a rig of floating line, strike indicator with weighted nymph and the line's depth adjusted to keep your fly a foot off the bottom will get you into the zone every time—this is usually the best system for cold-weather trout fishing.

There will be occasional glorious days during March when the temperature soars to 10°C—these are the times that a local Interior fly fisher needs to beg off work, phone in sick and hit the highway to the Crooked River. Expectations can be high for a hatch of Little Brown Stoneflies or midges, and what eager fly fisher can resist one of those opportunities when they are presented?

You can expect the emergence of insects to begin around 11 a.m. to 1 p.m. and last until 3 p.m. or so. You should arrive at the river at about 10 a.m., anticipating starting your day fishing a Hare's Ear Nymph (see p. 93), Little Brown Stonefly Nymph (see p. 81) or perhaps a Midge Larva (see p. 82).

Stonefly Patterns

Nymph

There are two stages of the stonefly life cycle available to trout: nymph and adult. When fishing a stonefly nymph imitation, it's important to know that the banks or close to them are the most productive spots to angle, because the nymph crawls along the bottom and climbs out of the stream to hatch. Stoneflies also love the rocky sections of a river, rarely inhabiting the slow, silt-laden stretches of a watercourse. Trout know this, and will be foraging these areas to capitalize on the nymph's vulnerability. With these thoughts in mind, fly fishers will have their best successes working slowly and quietly upstream along the banks, or bouncing a fly over and through boulder water, leading the drift of their retrieves to shoreline where a trout will follow and perhaps pounce on the offering with the glee of a bandit.

Adult

If a hatch of stoneflies is in progress, there will be small black or dark brown adult stoneflies present on the bank or in foliage along the river. A proven pattern for this hatch is the Elk Hair Caddis in sizes 14–18, or try my adult pattern, the Little Brown Stonefly (see p. 81). Although the model is called "brown," they are more commonly seen with black or smoky-grey colorations in northern streams.

Stonefly nymphs will begin their migration to shore during dusk in late evening or very early in the morning to avoid predator fish and ensure a healthy percentage survive for mating. Adults will attach to some sort of dry shoreline structure, a rock or branch, take a time-out rest period for their outer skin to dry and split, and then flit into foliage to hide and begin their search for a mate.

They survive for up to two weeks for their mating and nymph-laying rituals, leaving lots of opportunities for the wandering angler to take advantage of this act of nature. After mating, and when fertilized eggs have matured to tiny nymphs in the female's sac, she will return to the stream to drop her new progeny onto the water surface. Flying upstream, she spreads her wings and "kisses" the stream, depositing her nymphs in many places so the young are broadcast over a wide area, again maximizing their chances for survival.

Fish this pattern with a floating line, concentrating on rocky, boulder-strewn or gravel sections with moderate flow, working the fly upstream in likely seams fairly close to the shoreline, choice spots where the female will want to put down and place her young. I like to give my fly some intermittent action, twitching it occasionally with what I call the "Smith Skitter," a raising and wiggling of my rod tip to impart an intriguing "pop" to my fly, which has brought me a lot of fine trout over the years. And don't be afraid to fish a stonefly adult when you can't find any lurking around—trout in the North Country aren't that smart!

Midge Patterns

For winter trout fishing on the Crooked or any other northern river that has open water, the choices are simple: stonefly, midge or go home to a warm fire. The midge insect order is available to trout in three life cycle stages: larva or bloodworm, pupa and adult. Unlike stoneflies, midges and chironomids emerge from the water's surface. The hatch will be visible as the tiny insects launch and quickly fly away, like little aircraft on the wing.

Larvae

When there is no visible hatch present on an ice-cold river and a stonefly nymph won't bring results, your second choice is searching with sub-surface patterns like the Midge Larva (see p. 82), which lie in the muck zone of rivers, that layer of slime, algae and silt that covers gravel sections and tail-outs of pools. As you work your way through these spots with wading boots, many larvae are dislodged and float aimlessly down the river, which creates opportune possibilities for your buddy who is taking his turn at following your lead on this particular run of stream. Who said being first on the run is always better?

You can fish midge larvae with floating line, strike indicator set at twice the depth of the water you are working, and tight-tippet method, which means keep your leader to fly line connection taut at all times. If you prefer to not use an indicator (like me) you must use weighted flies, light fluorocarbon tippet (maximum 5-X), which sinks quickly, cast upstream so the path of the drift will exploit the maximum depth of the water and mend your dry line constantly to keep the fly in the deepest zone of the stream.

If you fish fast-flowing rivers (unlike the Crooked) with midge and nymph patterns, a sink-tip line can also be employed. My choices are a 1.5-m mini-tip, or using the system that I have taken to recently: Rio Versatip or Airflo lines armed with a selection of Airflo Poly Leaders, which are available in an array of lengths and sink rates to suit any fishing challenge. The leaders can be purchased separately, and are attached to the fly line with a loop-to-loop connection that allows you to change your entire depth set-up in minutes. Gone is the need for extra spools, a needle-knotted tapered leader to your fly line, and blood-knotting tippet to your leader, because the leaders also receive a short loop-to-loop connection of about 1.2–3 m of level tippet material. One line, one spool and dozens of options—hard to beat!

The take to a deeply fished larva pattern is very subtle, most often a slight stopping of the line as it bounces through the drift, and your response must be immediate or the offering is spit out like a bad sunflower seed. Strike often, at the slightest twitch, and you will be rewarded more times than not.

Midge larvae are available in a multitude of colours: bright red, maroon, olive, tan, cream and black. I have my best results with red and maroon colours, a hue that oxygen-starved worms will assume. Red works for me not only because I fish it the most, but I believe that red is a colour that fish see best, especially in the low light conditions of winter days. You should also tie them in olive for those days when you are confused and the fish are winning badly.

When you tie larva-type flies—segmented, several different colours, same pattern, wormy-looking appearance—one of the most difficult characteristics to achieve is movement. It's often the single most important factor between a productive pattern and a poor producer. Midge larvae don't have appendages or anything that resembles legs or feelers. However, adding a flowing hackle like pheasant or grouse will improve dead patterns, because their undulation simulates movement. Always consider "movement" when you design fly patterns, a lesson the late Jack Shaw taught me. There are many commercial larvae models on the market today; most look the same—lifeless. Try tweaking a few of them until you have something that replicates the following correct criteria: size, shape, colour and movement.

Pupae

If your midge larva pattern won't produce, it could be because the pupa phase of the insect is in staging mode on the streambed, receiving more attention from trout than larvae because of their nervous pre-emergence activity. There are many false starts—up again, down again—until gases forming in the pupa's body finally overwhelm the process and encased air forces the pupa to rise to the surface, culminating the transformation into adult.

It's only by experimentation that you can determine the best presentation method for your pupa imitation. If fish are taking the insect during the staging cycle, you will definitely need to be drifting your fly on the bottom of the stream using the same set-up as you fished the larva stage: floating line, weighted pattern and perhaps an indicator.

However, if you're lucky and conditions are right, the barometer is rising and the fish god is smiling on you, you may get a chance to get your fly off the riverbed and fish the ascending pupae. This activity calls for a dry line that is well greased to within 60 cm of the fly and the use of the "lift method" to simulate pupae on the move. You will achieve this "lift" by casting and mending upstream. As your line passes you and begins to swing, lift your rod tip; maintain tension through the rest of the drift and finish with a number of lift-and-settle manoeuvres of the fly, which can often produce startling results. Again, takes will be soft. You must strike at the slightest hesitation of leader, which you will see twitch before you will feel the fish take the hook.

Midge pupae are available in a variety of colours, the most common being grey, black, olive and sometimes blood red. The difference between midge and chironomid pupae is size—the midge is tied on hook sizes 16–20, chironomid 12–16. At the fly-tier's bench both insects can be tied in the same manner; however, I tend to use far less detail for my midge pupae patterns because they are so small. I try to keep them simple, concentrating on size, form and colour.

Emerger and Adult

What self-respecting fly fisher can pass up an opportunity to seduce trout to a surface fly when the temperature is only a few degrees above zero? "Not I," said the fly-fishing nut, especially after a long northern winter of snow clearing, whining studded tires, dead batteries and mucky roads. And yes, when conditions are right and the barometer is on a high cycle, those Crooked River trout will be looking up, God bless them, and if it isn't the little winter stonefly that arouses their interest, it'll for sure be the little midge that brings them to the surface to frolic and feed.

On those near-perfect winter days of 10°C that occur a few times in March, midge adults will begin to appear late morning, and continue to hatch until mid-afternoon when the warmth of day succumbs to the cool of lengthening shadows. It's a spurt of restless energy for the little insects, their moment in the sun, a chance to procreate and be counted amongst the many millions of midges that inhabit their special run of river. And the fly fishers wait patiently for their flash of glory, those split seconds of excitement that come when angler and trout connect. It matters not who wins the ensuing battle: for the fisher, the challenge has been met when the fish takes the lure; for the fish, happiness must surely be to live and rise once more to a fleeting hatch.

It's a little tricky to tell the difference between a "bulging" trout, one cruising under the surface grabbing emerging insects; a "smutting" fish, one that is sipping the tiniest of insects leaving only tiny rings; a "slasher," who takes big hoppers, stoneflies and travelling sedges on the run; and finally what we call the "plunger," the trout that dives on its prey and grabs the insect on the way up or on its re-entry. Having considered all this, what does it matter how a fish rises? What the fly fisher should really care about is that a fish is visibly feeding, and can be taken with a dry fly—the challenge of our sport gets no better than that.

Do we fish emerger or adult? This question can be debated until the cows come home. The answer, however, will never be clear and definitive. So why not a combination pattern, one that appears to imitate the trailing shuck of an emerger, but also offers a simulation of wing case, legs and body colour of the emerging adult? Our often-used Tom Thumb fits this profile admirably when fished in sizes 16 to 20, but I like to take it a little further down the trail and suggest a hybrid by tying my Midge Adult Emerger (see p. 83), which will take trout in all situations where midges are hatching.

If I have one fly to choose during a midge hatch, it will be this one. The water will be quiet tail water found at the end of slow pools. I will fish from below, working upstream from side to side with floating line, 2–3-m leader tapered to 5-X, and use short parachute casts that will only drift the fly drag-free for 3 m or so, and then take a step forward and repeat. The rise to the adult emerger will be a "smutting" or "sipping" variety, barely a dimple left to indicate the feeding, and the willing trout has taken your presentation. Tighten slowly, and the fish is yours.

A Day on the Crooked River

I had been eagerly watching the long-range forecast since mid-February, looking for a break in the cold front, searching for a day that would reach 5°C and perhaps trigger a wake-up response from the Crooked River trout. The day appeared on the computer screen, March 3, and a call to my retired friend and editor Bob Graham brought the "Sure, let's go!" response.

I had scouted the river a few weeks previous—it was in great condition, with waist-high snow on the banks. But the only road kept open to logging traffic this winter was the 200 Road, so we knew our fishing sections were limited to the 200 Bridge areas. However, it was a glorious day: bright sun, warmth, good company and easy wading after a long winter—a good recipe for an outing regardless of the outcome.

We cautiously worked our way upriver from the bridge on the west bank, taking the inside track to the good corner hole, picking our way through the frigid water in search of a few spots to find some feeding trout. Heck, I thought, even whitefish would do the trick today—it's sure nice to be alive and fishing once again.

I left Bob working the corner pool, and continued wading upriver, watching for signs of trout, eyes up... And then it happened—a slip on a log and a half-dunk on one side up to my neck half-filled my waders. Damn cold, that river—I was christened on my first outing of the year, not twenty minutes into it. Nothing could be done about it, but wring out three layers of clothing, shrug it off and get back in the water. Usually the optimist, I spent the rest of the day tracking toward sunlight, staying out of the shade, hoping my clothes would dry out, which never happened... and neither did the fish, for me.

Bob was top rod that day, picking off several nice rainbows to 40 cm on a peacock nymph—I didn't tell him about the mishap until we finished for the day. He too had a christening—the handsome little 4-weight rod I built for him over the winter. A superb outing, a toast from the flask of good Irish whiskey to the Crooked River, and another day well spent.

Cutthroat on the Kitimat

When work beckons me to the northwest, even in winter, it is worthwhile taking a fly rod because I can always target some species of fish: resident cutthroat and Dolly Varden year round, winter-run steelhead in early spring, sockeye and spring salmon in summer and coho and summer-run steelhead in fall.

If you get to know a few local people in the sport shops and drop a dollar or two in their stores now and then, you'll gather local information on spots where fishing can be productive, even during a summer or fall blow-out, because a few river systems in the northwest—the Kitimat and Lakelse, for example—are not affected by heavy rains, or are capable of clearing quickly.

The Kitimat is a beautiful little stream to fish, not as forbidding as the Skeena, and can be worked with a pontoon or drift boat for its entire length from the Hwy 37 Bridge to the river's estuary at Minette Bay in Douglas Channel. It does change, however, and can be blocked with a sweeper at any time because of the enormous fir and cottonwood trees that line its banks. Your best bet is to always drift with a buddy, wear a personal floatation device and keep your eyes one corner ahead as you drift.

The river can be accessed from Hwy 37 Bridge by pulling into any of the many side roads leading off to the right (west) from the highway. Many have pull-offs and parking close to the road (if you drive a BMW), and trail access to the Kitimat. Most main paths can be navigated with a pickup truck, but are narrow, usually wet and can be slippery coming out if the weather is foul during your day on the river. If you pontoon the river and only have one vehicle, a common practice is to drive upriver from town, park and unload, pontoon down and call a cab on your cellphone from Cable Car Run to pick you up at the Haisla Bridge in Radley Park, then return to your vehicle and come back for your boat.

A Day on the Kitimat

On March 25 the afternoon beckoned me to stretch the legs and try for cutthroat and dollies on the Kitimat, which was in perfect condition. My friend and customer John Heinonkari had been begging me to find the time for a year; finally we could fulfill the promise. Marcus Feldhoff, who works for the federal Department of Fisheries in Kitimat, and Dan Siepman joined us. Our plan was to drive upstream and enter above the power-line run, where Dan had run into a slew of trout the previous week. We thought we might get lucky and hit winter-run steelhead, which had just begun to enter the river to spawn before freshet in May—our 5-weight tackle would be challenged if that event occurred.

It was raining and overcast as we drove ten minutes upriver, entered the power-line access road, parked and made a twenty-five-minute hike down the path, coursing along the old river channel the Kitimat gouged out when it turned several years ago in a big flood. As we wandered beside the former waterway, pools appeared, remnants of runoff from high water, fed by creeks, springs and winter rains. In the ponds, thousands of small

alevin, recently emerged from the gravel beds, protected from the main ·
river currents by the pool, scattered as we walked by.

It was a joyous walk, full of anticipation, alive with the chatter of good
company, wondering what the day would bring. Are the trout still there?
Are we going to be first, or is someone else aware of the river's pleasures?
Has the river dropped enough from the previous days' rains to cross safely?
We arrived at the run, sized it up, crossed and entered a long glide of soft
water that's prime holding territory for the cutthroat and Dolly Varden we
searched for that day.

It had been twenty years since I last targeted coastal cutthroat and
wandered the sloughs of the mighty Fraser, the soft Nicomen Slough backwaters, the Stave outflow and the wide beaches of the Harrison, searching
for elusive cutts that can appear one day and be 30 km upriver the next. I
reminisced that I hadn't tied a cutthroat pattern since 1992 when I moved
north, and casually surveyed my tattered old flies. I pondered aloud, "Tom
Murray's Rolled Muddler (see p. 84) will work—it's been around since
the '60s; the Silver Doctor will work—that's an old standby; also the Egg-
n-Eye (see p. 84). Mine don't look too good after all those years—I'll use
some given to me by John."

We knew the trout would be looking for salmon fry, alevin recently
emerged from the gravel, yolk-sacs still intact. It was floating line or short
sink-tip time: 4-X tippets, 3-m leaders and 5-weight outfits. The minnow
patterns we chose are standard fare for the Kitimat River: silver Mylar bodies, sparse brown underwing, some polar or crystal flash for the overwing
and a short red throat to simulate the yolk-sac.

And what an afternoon we had! The trout were still there, lying in soft
corner water, passed over by the small flotilla of pontoon boats that had
drifted through shortly before we arrived. As the day progressed the rain
ceased and the sun appeared. The water warmed and trout came up steadily
for the minnow offerings, over fifty of them, cutts and dollies between 30
and 45 cm: beautifully marked fish, clean, bright and silver—all released.

That was March fishing at its very best: good company, fine trout fishing, unspoiled scenery and another northern day to remember.

April: Rain, Sun and Open Lakes

Finally, the sun feels warm and inviting. By mid-month, most of the snow below 700 m is gone; no longer do we get evening frosts; the ground is mostly thawed, but still too cold for planting or digging. Later in the month, as April progresses into longer days and the sun strengthens, countless birds arrive daily. Yellow warblers with their happy, glorious trills delight us on spring days. Rufous and ruby-throated hummingbirds flit from feeder to feeder, replenishing energy lost from their long, perilous 10,000-km journeys from as far south as Panama and South America. Robins have come earlier, and are tending their first batches of sky-blue eggs. A male willow grouse has been drumming for a mate every morning, beginning at first light—he'll likely get caught by a fox if he keeps giving up his cover! Life is good once more for creatures living in the north.

"April showers bring May flowers." For the fly fisher, heavy rains open lakes in a hurry when puddles of water form on top of the melting ice, adding weight and speeding rot from the surface down more rapidly than heat generated from the sun can penetrate the ice-cover. Once lakes begin to open along the shoreline, it's usually a week to complete ice-off. A strong wind or two during this opening period further aids the process, pushing free water over the ice floe, gradually winning the battle and freeing the lake from its icy grasp.

The first week to ten days after ice-out can be very good fishing, followed by what is termed spring turnover, a complete mixing of a lake's water column. Sometimes this mixing happens over a few days and clears quickly, but most times fishing is poor for a week or two until the methane dissipates and the oxygen content stabilizes. Lower elevation lakes open first; eager-beaver fly fishers can follow ice-off to their favourite lakes during the month of April and well into May simply by travelling to higher-elevation lakes every week. Once all your pet lakes are ice-free, it's time to reacquaint yourself with lower-elevation lakes, which will be in prime spring fishing condition because insect hatches are a month ahead of the highest lakes.

Insect hatch activity, which is highly dependent on water temperature, is affected by the elevation of lakes. The hatches will travel with you as you ascend to higher-elevation lakes, beginning with midges and chironomids; followed by the mayflies; then damselflies, caddis, and dragonflies; and finally, in late summer, the nuptial flights of water boatmen. Again, the trick to maximizing hatch activity is to follow them up and down the mountains, using the same logic you used to escape spring turnover. Of course, when there is no hatch activity, you can always depend on the ever-reliable scuds and leeches to satisfy your fish-catching hunger.

Lakes of the North Country are stubborn when it comes to shedding their ice cover, but I'm ever the optimist that Dragon Lake will be open mid-April and grant me a few fishing trips before Eena, Vivian and Tory lakes open around the end of the month.

Rivers also present fly-fishing opportunities. Although spring snowmelt is muddying the waters a little, open-water streams like the Crooked River fish well during April because its elevation is consistent for the 90-km length of the system with no major feeder tributaries entering to affect its flow. Rivers with more gradient like the Willow, Bowron and Parsnip, although fishable and exempt from spring closure, are beginning their freshet and are too coloured to be worthwhile trying until the water levels begin to drop around mid-June. The Nechako, however, is dam-regulated and worth a try in its upper reaches above Fort Fraser, around

Pelicans stop for a rest on their way north. Dragon Lake, Cariboo. Glenn Gerbrandt photo.

Wilkins Park in the Miworth area west of Prince George and also at the mouth of McMillan Creek in the city.

Dragon Lake

My fishing buddy Dale Freschi and I eagerly anticipate an email from our friend Kevin Crawford, who lives on Dragon Lake in Quesnel, with the note announcing the ice has come off the big lake, which holds chunky rainbows up to 7 kg. For the fly fisher, Dragon is the earliest worthwhile lake to open in the North Cariboo–Central Interior. Once it is ice-free, Dragon is the lake that we try to get onto several times during the first ten days of opening. We check with Kevin daily to get reports on how the water looks and when to expect spring turnover, which is the signal to vacate Dragon for a week to ten days, and begin looking for my favourite early lakes around Prince George to open: Cobb, Eena, Vivian and perhaps Tory.

Early spring fly fishing at Dragon can range from fair to spectacular. Some years the lunkers are happy to see you; other years they are not.

And I suppose that's why they call it "fishing"—if it were always spectacular, everyone would be doing it, right? And what's the fun in fishing with a crowd?

Dragon Lake is situated on Hwy 97 South, just past the outskirts and south of the city of Quesnel. You don't need a four-wheel drive to visit Dragon Lake. A car-topper with your boat, pontoon boat or canoe, or a trailer and boat will do nicely, and there is public access at several spots on the lake. Access is free at the large public boat launch on the east side of the lake, and also free at a small launch just west of Robert's Roost Campsite and RV Park, though parking is limited to only a few vehicles. The RV park at Robert's Roost charges a small fee for public launching, as does Legion Beach in the northeast corner and the private campsite at the southeast corner of the lake.

All the 225 hectares and 6 km of Dragon Lake is a fishery. Some spots, because of their bottom structures, slopes and flats, are better than others, but fish can generally be found everywhere. With its maximum depth of 8 m and mean of 7 m, the lake has a very uninteresting and uniform bottom profile, but produces weed growth throughout the entire system; hence an aquatic smorgasbord of unequalled proportions is available to trout, and a quality fishery that arguably has no rival in British Columbia. Although not known for the table fare of its rainbow trout, the Dragon Lake stock can pack on a half kilogram of weight per year. It's not unusual for a 30-cm spring trout of half a kilogram to be 40 cm and 1.5 kg by late fall due to the fantastic growth spurts that this amazing factory affords its fish.

Dragon is normally stocked annually with 25–50,000 wild yearling Blackwater/Dragon strain from its hatchery program. Several years ago the lake was tested with triploids, which are developed from eggs of both genders that are shocked to generate sterile fry that will not go through the reproductive process, but instead concentrate on growth, producing exceptionally large trout in prime rearing ecosystems like Dragon. Dale Freschi and I caught a few of those 60-cm-plus silver torpedoes in 2009; they were approaching 4 kg in their fourth year. In 2010 and 2011, we released several 5-kg rainbows—Dragon has once more become quite a fishery, with 50-cm trout becoming the norm and making up one-half of your catch.

Dragon can be a moody lake, as are most "big fish" lakes. Otherwise it would be barren of fish because it is a city lake with ten thousand people living in close proximity, and another ten thousand who would like to live there. The north half of Dragon is ringed with year-round residences; some were built fifty years ago, many more are recent. How many can boast about living on a freshwater lake that provides a fly fisher a chance to release up to twenty 2–3-kg rainbows in a good day of fishing?

The lake fishes well for trollers with gear or flies because of its bathymetric shape. For the fly fisher who loves to anchor, however, there are many prime areas where trout will congregate. The key to success at Dragon is to locate moving fish—trout that are foraging and showing on the surface, or visibly moving onto shoal zones. These are fish that are feeding aggressively and can be caught. Sometimes they are moving in the middle of the lake, which is where you should fish them, because in my experience they will usually stay at that comfortable depth for the day.

During early spring before lake turnover, your best bet is to fish the edges in shallow water, right into the bulrushes if necessary—these are the areas that are warming the fastest, carry the most oxygen and will capture the spring migrations of insects as they travel shoreward from their winter habitats.

Dragon is laden with shore structure that attracts fish. Typical spots to anchor your watercraft are points of land, small bays, creek mouths, islands with drop-offs, and long shelves. If you are observant while working these areas thoroughly and vary your tactics, retrieves, patterns and depths, you will soon discover secrets of success by trial and elimination and become a better fly fisher.

Let's discuss some of the best spots that consistently produce trout at Dragon. If fish are going to move into an area to feed, these are the places they will gather, and if you're lucky and observant, you'll be there when they come in.

Legion Beach

At the north end of the lake on the east side is Legion Beach, which is a Royal Canadian Legion-sponsored camp with a private dock and several recreational vehicle campsites available to the public. You can also fish

A soon-to-be-released trout gets her photo taken. Glenn Gerbrandt photo.

Legion Beach by launching free of charge at the public dock and taking a short journey up the lake.

The small bay at this end is quite shallow, weedy and set up with a bowl type of structure, where trout tend to circle the rim, venture onto the edges, shelves and into the rushes on their travels during heavy feeding, then come together in the middle during the more intense light of midday.

Throughout the area, as in all prime spots in Dragon Lake, there are dense weed patches that have interspersed random circles and bottom zones that are free of weed cover—these are the best fishing places in the neighbourhood. You'll see them quite easily, because the floor is white marl, contrasting with the deep olive green of ever-present weed beds. Anchor and fish these choice places carefully, concentrating on presenting your offering in the bottom zone, unless fish are showing.

Public Boat Launch

Continuing along Dragon Lake Road on the east side of Dragon's north end, you'll soon come to the public boat launch, where you can put all sizes of boats into the lake and park free of charge for the day. It's a busy spot, but has a solid concrete launch site suitable for large water craft. If your vessel is motorized, you can cover the entire lake from this launch site, or you can concentrate on this north half of the lake and likely have as good luck here as anywhere else, sometimes better.

During early spring, lots of spawning trout will be hovering around the boat launch because of its gravel bottom. Some people take pleasure in targeting these poor-quality trout, but my preference is to leave them be. Most will survive the rigours of the spawn ritual and live to be silver trophies once again, but their chances are slim if they are hooked and harassed repeatedly while they are seeking to dump their eggs and recuperate.

The first spot to try is the small corner bay south of the boat launch, where there are usually a number of good trout hanging around. Farther along this shoreline, the mouth of Hallis Creek and its bay are closed to fishing between the signs to protect spawning trout near the hatchery and egg-collection station.

The exposed island directly across from the boat launch is another good area for trout to congregate. Working the points of islands is always good practice when you are looking for holding spots—trout will creep onto the shelves and slide back into deep water cover quickly. First, you should anchor in shallow water and cast to the far shore, working your pattern from deep pockets to the shelf, and then side to side across the ledge to maximize the potential of your stay. If a wind is blowing, look to drop anchor on the lee side of the island, and cast to the edge of the riffle created by the wind; often trout are looking for food drifting with current produced by turbulence—another method to maximize your opportunities to tangle with a hog fish.

Robert's Roost Area

The point and bay in front of Robert's Roost Campsite is another area of prime holding water, and the spot where in October 1992 I caught my largest Interior rainbow to date, 73 cm long and over 4 kg. That rainbow looked like a steelhead, but it was nothing compared to the one that my old friend, Bob McNichols, caught on the same day, same trip to Dragon: 86 cm and over 7 kg! When Bob held the fish across his arms, its full head and tail were well past his shoulder width. The trout was caught on the west side of the aforementioned island while Bob was fast-trolling a blood leech. Was it luck or skill? Doesn't matter, he was in the right place at the right time with the right lure, and caught the largest rainbow trout I've ever seen taken from a lake.

Moving west along the shoreline from Robert's Roost, you'll discover a shallow shelf several hundred metres long lined with year-round residences—this is another place where trout will venture from deep holding water to cruise the ledge in search of their daily intake of protein. The fish won't show much in this area but you should be prepared to give it a half-hour workover if you are travelling by.

Directly across from the point at Robert's Roost, there is a small bay on the south shore that always deserves a good look before venturing into the south end of the lake. Again, park on the edge of the transition zone to deep water and fish your pattern from deep to shallow by casting to the far shore.

South End

My friends and I fish the south end more than any other area of Dragon Lake, not only because it's near our friend Kevin's home and we get to say hello and have up-to-date fishing information, but also because we don't think it's worth our time to zoom all over the lake trying to find moving fish; the logic here is to keep your fly in the water, watch for activity and usually good things will eventually happen. We launch at the private campsite for five bucks a head, where caretaker friend, John, guards the gate, and can be moving and fishing any part of the productive areas of the south end within ten minutes. There are four main hot spots at this end of the lake: Mayfly Bay, Goose Point, Big Boy Bay and Pump House.

Mayfly Bay is aptly named by Kevin Crawford, and encompasses the small bay area of the northeast corner of the south end. Depending on ice-off date and water temperature, the Callibaetis mayfly hatch will begin 4–6 weeks later, and this bay will be bubbling with 1–3-kg trout that under the right conditions will not hesitate to take a well-presented dry fly. The mayfly hatch will continue sporadically for another 4–6 weeks until the water warms. This usually doesn't factor into April fishing days, but I'm not saying it couldn't...

Mayfly Bay is a wonderful place to anchor and fish because of the variety of structure it presents: a long weed-covered shelf with several hundred metres of 1–2-m water depth; a transition zone of 3–4 m deep leading to the shelf; and opportunities to fish right into the shoreline bulrushes for cruising rainbows.

While you fish the bay in April, wistfully dreaming about those dry-fly days that etch our memories forever, take solace in the fact that this bay is a great spot early in the year to fish the early migrating insects, leeches and scuds, and is always a safe bet to anchor and present your midge and chironomid patterns.

Immediately west of Mayfly Bay is an area we call Goose Poop Point, named because of the nesting Canadas and their baggage, which envelopes another small bay, a point of land and drop-off to 8 m of water and a long shelf north of the point. Trout cruise along the north shelf and gather to spread out into the bay and along the corner, often milling in this area throughout the day. It's a popular place and often gets congested with anchored craft, but is always a good bet and a prime spot to pick a scrap with one of Dragon's bruisers. Both properties in the area are private docking facilities; visitors are encouraged to respect this fact and not enter or use the lands for any means, including relieving yourself.

Looking directly west across the lake from Goose Point you'll see Big Boy Bay, another very small inlet bay that is worth a look if you're having trouble picking up a fish anywhere else, and it'll likely be a big one. Trout move into these bays to feed and cruise the shelves and grasses for easy pickings, so be cognizant of any irregular structures when fishing for lunkers in Dragon; they seek them out, and so should you!

Finally, the very south end called Pump House is yet another gathering place for fish. It's a very shallow bay, only 1–2 m deep, with the pumphouse on your right or west side of the cove, that will transition into about 4–5-m depth past the mouth of the inlet. On grey days, fish will move right into the cove; on bright days they tend to hang out in deeper water along the edge. Many anglers will park and work this bay all day, waiting patiently for their hour or two of superb trout fishing that may or may not come to them on a typical outing at Dragon.

April Fly Patterns

Lake water after ice-off is cold, around 3–4°C; not very inviting for fish, humans or wildlife of any sort, so you can't blame the trout for not cooperating—they're in shock mode trying to find oxygenated water. In some cases shallow lakes can be very vulnerable to a "spring kill" if the lake's water is infused with methane gas by strong wind which mixes the water layers too rapidly at ice-off, resulting in no pockets of oxygenated liveable water for fish.

When the fish won't play, it's not a good idea to give yourself a hard time either; after all, we fish because we love to fish, and trying to coax a winter-weary trout into a tussle is only half the challenge of fly fishing. The other half is keeping warm and dry, thankful we don't have to live submerged in frigid water like our friend, the trout.

Spring fly patterns for any still-water lake in April are limited to several insects and their families: midges, chironomids, shrimp or scuds, leeches and water boatmen. Some, like scuds and leeches, are preferred diet items in early spring; often you will find trout selective to only these food organisms, exclusive of any other, for short periods of time before strong midge hatches develop with warming spring water. For some fly fishers, chironomids are the *only* flies they use year-round, oblivious to whatever else is going on that arouses the trout. For me, I rank scud, leech and bloodworm patterns above chironomids during April, these choices waning as May brings warmer water temperatures, prolific midge hatches and more favourable barometer readings.

Scud (Freshwater Shrimp)

Scuds are the mainstay of the diets of many freshwater organisms in the ecosystems of Interior lakes. Not only do they sustain all species of fish, they also supply the protein source for other insects larger than themselves: damsel and dragonfly nymphs, leeches and backswimmers. They are probably the most symbiotic organism in a still-water environment, feeding on plant, insect and animal matter with little mayfly nymphs comprising the bulk of their preferred food palates.

Central Interior fly fishers often overlook the lowly scud because many of our favourite ponds and lakes are slightly acidic, low in calcium content and not great scud-producing environments, but a weed-laden body of water like Dragon has billions upon billions of the little crustaceans. They probably comprise up to 30 percent of a typical Dragon Lake trout's nutrients. Drag up a bagful of Dragon's weed on your anchor, and you'll be impressed with the quantity and quality of the insect life living there—most of your catch will be shrimp along with a smattering of leeches, bloodworms and mayfly and damsel nymphs.

There are two species of scud in our Interior waters, *Gammarus* and *Hyalella*. The larger *Gammarus* is the dominant species in calcium-rich lakes like Dragon; the little *Hyalella* is prolific in both types of still water, but are the principal shrimp of clear, high-elevation and acidic, tannin-coloured ponds of the Central Plateau.

Although I have not fished scud patterns very often since moving to the Central Interior in 1992 and they rest unused in my old fly box, I regard them fondly because they gave me many memorable days when I fished them religiously during the 1970s while living in Kamloops. Since that time, when many fly patterns were originated and improved upon by Jack Shaw and others, many adaptations have been made on standard patterns. In the case of the scud, it has become the "baggy" shrimp model, replacing the Werner Shrimp's deer-hair back with plastic strip and its palmer-hackled legs with picked-out dubbing.

Call me a traditionalist fly tier if you will; I think I've earned the reputation—I believe the sliver of plastic is a good idea to imitate a shell-back. I use it because it's much more durable than deer hair, but I still like the looks of palmered hackle for a scud's legs. It better imitates the wiggle and scurry of a typical shrimp, captures light, and is alive with contrast when compared to picked-out dubbing material.

In Dragon Lake *Gammarus* shrimp are dark olive or yellow, camouflaged with the colour of weed growth, and can be fished in an array of sizes from a humongous #8 hook to one as minute as a #16, owing to the multi-brooded scud's ability to produce offspring throughout the year. Every lake will have its own colour of shrimp, but the three colours I work with are dark olive-brown, golden yellow and pale chartreuse green for my smallest imitations and the *Hyalella* species.

Shrimp are like rabbits in the animal world—they produce huge litters and feed a lot of predators. A consideration when tying and fishing scud patterns is that you must lighten your body colour with the juveniles—an olive green adult will be pale chartreuse when first born and into its early teenage years, only a few short months in the life of a humble scud.

Fish shrimp patterns with a floating line when anchored in less than 3 m of water, a full-sinking line in 3 to 6 m. Weight them well to get them down and fish them with a slow hand-twist retrieve, varying your pace and stopping often to rest, very similar to the crawling action of an emerging chironomid: twitch, draw a few inches, rest awhile, start over—fish on!

Leeches

There is no question that leeches are a favourite table fare for fish early in the year. The mature insect is on the prowl just after ice-off, checking out decayed weed beds for its favourite meal of scuds, snails and small nymphs, and more importantly, looking for a mate.

If I had to choose only one fly for April, it would be a leech type of fly: a Micro Leech (see p. 87), Bulldog (pp. 87–88), Olive Seal Bugger or one of my Blood Bugger patterns (p. 86)—they just seem to be the ticket for spring water after ice-off when the water temperature hovers below 10°C. Trout are shocked and lethargic, and even the fly fisher struggles to keep warm. The reason leeches are dominant after the ice goes out is because they love to dine on decaying matter and dead plant vegetation, and the abundance of their favourite insects in early spring and the warming water is the perfect combination for them to reactivate their life cycles.

For the fly fisher who loves to fish chironomids in early spring, leeches and chironomids work well together, usually after the intense hatches of midges and chironomids is over for the day—trout love to pack a few leeches into their gullets after a big meal of little bugs.

Ever since I began fly fishing back in the late 1960s, leeches have been my "save the skunking" patterns. If I was desperate in late afternoon after a poor morning, I always found I could get even with the fish by rigging a #3 full-sink line and going deep along a drop-off to rouse a good trout into taking a poke at a Shaw leech pattern. I haven't used Jack's patterns for a number of years, not because they won't work, but more because of the advent of improved fly-tying materials. I think there are better and more realistic choices now than those available in the 1950s and '60s when Jack was inventing his staple fly patterns. Many of the new dubbing materials have incorporated glitter in their fibres, which adds life, translucence and that hard-to-find slimy, buggy look.

Leeches are well represented by a variety of fly patterns, many that have been around for fifty or sixty years—for example, Careys, woolly buggers, woolly worms and yes, for real old-timers, even Doc Spratleys. They are some of the simplest flies to learn to tie, great for teaching students a few uncomplicated steps toward being competent fly tiers and, most importantly, will catch fish no matter how bad they look to yourself or the public.

Leeches move in a slow and steady undulating manner, which is why 10–12 wraps of lead wire added to the front half of your imitations is a good idea. It allows your fly to bob in the water, replicating the manner in which a leech picks its way around weed beds and free-swims in the water column. Instead of lead weight, many fly tiers use gold, silver or orange tungsten beads when they tie leech patterns, which also provide the weight to allow the pattern to undulate. I have never seen a leech that looked like it had a bead head, but they do work, and it is said "the proof is always in the pudding."

Depending on the pattern and depth of the lake, a leech is normally best fished deeply, on the bottom with a full-sink line using a slow hand-crawl retrieve, or if you are anchored and standing, with long, slow arm-length pulls of your fly line. Some of the impressionistic leech imitations, for example, Brent Schlenker's popular Bulldog (see p. 87) pattern or Denny Rickard's Olive Seal Bugger, which imitate everything from bait fish to leeches and damsel nymphs, are most productive when fished with a fast-strip retrieve. Defying all fishing logic, however, micro leech models are often fished with indicators in a comatose fashion, similar to the method many people fish chironomid patterns. My personal opinion is that trout actually take them for chironomids, not leeches.

I use many colours for leeches. Unfortunately they all work, but not usually at the same time, so deciding which leech to use is often hit and miss.

I often begin a pattern like my Blood Bugger Leech (see p. 86) in size #8 or 10 and proceed to change colours from there. Alternative body materials and marabou tail colours I use are: Dragonfly Mohair Plus Black-Red with black tail; Arizona Simi Blood Leech with claret tail; Dazzle Dubbing BC Blood with black tail; Stillwater Sparkle Blend Maroon with purple tail; and finally, for an olive leech, Stillwater Soft Blend Olive with olive tail.

Midge and Chironomid

Midges? Dare I write about midges and chironomid in the same paragraph? I think the pesky midge has defied and wreaked eternal havoc on more lake fishers than any other insect. The only good thing about pairing these two bugs is that their main hatches occur at the same times of year, spring and fall.

When the midge is a solitary hatch, trout are very difficult to entice. The most difficult challenge is the size of the insect, a diminutive 1–2 mm in length. Take a look at a ruler; these are tiny, tiny flies, usually olive of the chaoborus or glass worm species and impossible to replicate on a hook. If you are lucky enough to somehow catch a random fish and examine its stomach contents, and discover the gullet is packed with thousands of green transparent larvae and pupae, you are in for a tough day. Your best bet is to choose an olive micro leech or chironomid, hoping colour is part of the attraction and trout can be fooled.

Chironomids, however, are the most staple hatch to occur in early spring, beginning soon after ice-off, continuing their activity well into the months of May and June depending on water temperature, waning in July and August, and then coming on again during September and October. I sheepishly admit that I am not a diehard fisher of chironomid, preferring to seek my spring game with bloodworm, leech, scud and mayfly nymph, resorting to chironomids when I have to or am being badly beaten and out-fished by anchored, bobber-slinging chironomid guys and gals.

I must explain that last statement or people will think I am an old fuddy-duddy. I began my passion for fly fishing in 1968 and moved to Kamloops in 1972 where I befriended the late Jack Shaw, who taught me fly tying and how to fish chironomids with type 1 slow-sink and type 2 medium-sink fly line choices using the countdown method: cast a long line and let it sink for five, ten, fifteen or twenty seconds before you begin your slow inch-by-inch retrieve. Once you hit fish at their preferred depth, you have the formula, and you should be off to the races if the trout want to play. Without the bobber, you feel every touch through your rod, and can enjoy the scenery and wildlife while you fish instead of concentrating on watching the bobber—it's just something I prefer.

Chironomids have four life stages: egg, larva (bloodworm), pupa and adult. After hatching, all three phases can be deadly to imitate, but the pupa stage is the one most fly fishers concentrate on because it's the most visible and vulnerable form for the fish. The pupa ascends through the water column at a slow, meandering pace, wriggling and swimming its way to freedom on the surface, pausing and drifting through resting periods, gradually finishing its long, treacherous journey at the top. Even then it's a target for cruising trout—it can't be free until it breaks the surface film, sheds its shuck and dries its wings for ten to twenty seconds, at which time it's a meal item for quick-winged cliff swallows and frisky trout that are pillaging the surface water. Life can be tough when you are an insect!

A Little April Glory—Dragon Lake

Dragon opened early in 2010, the last of its ice dropping in a March 29 windstorm, which is several weeks earlier than normal and a month ahead of 2009. Alas, an early opening doesn't always provide for great fishing. Perhaps the trout are as confused as we are, similar to us rising at 5 a.m. when we are accustomed to getting up at 7 a.m. Whatever the reason or excuse to fish, it's never a bad idea to round up a few buddies and *just go* no matter what the prospects, outcomes or thought processes. You can chart the weather, barometric pressure, moon position and solunar tables that will predict favourable weather, a rising barometer and the best days of the month and time of day to fish, but what does this mean unless you are retired, live on a lake or river and are available to take advantage of every opportunity to capture great trout fishing? Not a darn thing—the best time to go fishing is when you can—to hell with the reasons not to! We live and play in a great land of opportunity in this North Country—why not exploit our moments every chance we get?

Kevin Beatty is a good sport. He'll freeze his tail off in a pontoon boat during early trout fishing season any possible chance he can get, but I prefer my newly acquired one-man 10-foot punt when the water temperature is hovering in the low single digits. A pontoon boat is a huge step above a belly boat through early spring because you only get wet from your knees down, but after thirty-plus years of spring fishing in those styles of watercraft, I must admit the punt is pretty comfortable. In reality, a serious fly fisher needs to own all three watercraft: a punt for easy access on boat launch-style lakes; a pontoon boat for four-wheel drive access lakes and river drifting; and a belly or U-boat for hike-in lakes.

Dragon was tough fishing after ice-off. Not for Kevin Crawford who lives on the lake and can watch and wait for the trout to move, but for regular working guys like me who can't afford to retire, own lakefront property, or even dream of living on a fishing lake with my wife unless it has ski-boat potential (usually poor fishing prospects). Kevin Beatty and I fished it April 4; Kevin, Blair Moffat and I tried it April 11; and the three of us joined by Dale Freschi fished it on April 18.

During a day of fishing, Dragon rainbows do not go onto a bite for long periods of time unless they have good reason such as bug activity— the first strong chironomid or mayfly hatch of the season; a very favourable barometer with an upswing in air temperature; or a positive lunar phase, preferably new moon or first quarter. Some or any of these conditions do not occur on a regular basis, usually only several times during a calendar month, which is why fishing can be great one week and fair, average or poor the next. The fish are still there but their conditions, habitat and feeding cycles are constantly changing, which is why we hear "Good luck" from friends and family as we head out the door to enjoy some of our favourite days on earth. In my line of thinking, serious fisher people should not have a regular work week. We should be able to work when *we* want to, like maybe two days a week, but getting paid for five would be nice.

When you catch a big Dragon Lake trout and have the tackle and awareness to survive the strike, you know immediately that you have a strong trout on the line. There is rarely a long heart-stopping surface run; rather, a gruelling slug-it-out, give-and-take battle with a fish you know is a bruiser: large shoulders, heavy girth and the muscles of a warrior. Kevin

Crawford and Dale Freschi are the best I know for enticing these beasts of Dragon Lake—I've caught a few monsters, but these two guys are uncanny when it comes to kicking the butts of rainbows over 60 cm long. These trout are so strong that Dale uses 1-X or 2-X strength leaders to humble them (Dale likes to play, tire and release his fish quickly); I prefer 3-X or 4-X tippets, but use a moderate action 5-weight rod with lots of forgiving bend because I like to play my trout. Dragon Lake trout are not leader-shy, because Dale will regularly out-fish me using heavy test leaders. So much for the theory of light leaders for big trout because they are spooky!

We picked up some nice trout this spring, the largest 70 cm in the 5-kg class. Brian Chan, friend and retired biologist, fostered the plan to stock triploids (sterile male and female genders) in Dragon a few years ago, and it appears the program is going to be very successful in producing *very* large chrome trout that will live a few years longer, concentrate on growth and generate monsters that we hope will give us some fish in the 80-cm and 6-kg range before they die off. Those are trout I'm looking forward to catching, or let's say hooking first.

May: Warmer Days Are Coming

Ah, but the Central Interior weather in May is a zephyr one day and a howling north wind the next! For the first few weeks of the month, depending on whether it continues to freeze at night, our low-elevation lakes struggle to become ice-free, opening along the shoreline during the above-zero temperatures of midday, and then quietly closing up again at night. Some years, these spring cold spells can persist for weeks, and it's frustrating for anxious fly fishers who are impatiently waiting for their personal freedom. After enduring another winter season in the north, we deserve to feel the warm sun on our backs!

The variety of birdlife that arrives in the north during May is nothing short of spectacular. Robins have been around since the last snows of March and are working on their second batch of offspring by late June, but it's the arrival of yellow warblers, brightly coloured western tanagers, finches and rufous hummingbirds that signal fine spring weather is just around the corner. If you are lucky enough to be on their flyway, the arrival of Canada geese as ponds and lakes open for their breeding grounds is a clatter of life in itself, followed by lonesome loons, chattering ducks, mergansers, sandhill cranes and always the graceful trumpeter swans that have been welcome bystanders through the cold winter.

In the realm of an impatient fly fisher, eventually all things come to pass: lakes shed their winter cover and rivers burst with renewed energy; nature responds once more to the beckoning of spring and the fishing season begins. April has been toying with our emotions by allowing us some early fleeting moments of fishing madness, but now it's May. The *real* trout season is almost upon us and we begin to search our home waters in earnest for intense bug hatches. In lakes, chironomid, midge and mayfly are awakening, and the ever-present meat and potatoes of our lakes are also begging our fly lines for a chance: leeches, scuds and bloodworms.

Rivers and streams are in runoff stage, blowing through their home valleys with reckless abandon, scouring and purging their banks and bottoms, rearranging and renewing everything in their paths. If winter has left a healthy snowpack and if heavy spring rains have come suddenly and strong, moving waters once placid and calm become raging torrents, spectacles that sometimes alter their environments forever. Peak runoff time is normally late May to the first week of June; with a few exceptions, it will be late June before we can target trout in our river systems, but there are opportunities.

May is an interesting month for fly fishers in the north. Our average daily maximum temperature during May is 16°C, the average low 3°C. Precipitation is minimal, the fourth-lowest month of the year, even less than each of the summer months. But the weather can change suddenly. It's not unusual to get caught in a spring snowstorm while fishing lakes and streams. It's also not remarkable to have a few days that soar into the mid-20s.

The ultimate, perfect May for me as a fly fisher for lakes under 1,000-m elevation will feature ice-off and turnover the last two weeks of April, with lakes clearing the first week of May and daytime temperatures averaging in the high teens with a few days of 20°C thrown in for good hatches and suntanning weather for my wife, Lois. Further, all of my days off will be the best solunar days of the month, the barometer will be high, the winds light and trout will rise to eat my dry flies... in my dreams, an ideal May.

Alas, our natural world is always in transition, rarely perfect. A fly fisher is forever subjected to the whims of nature, and we must learn to adjust our thinking and observations to what we are given. For example, a cold spring

Morning mist on Roche Lake, Kamloops area. Glenn Gerbrandt photo.

delays the oncoming hatches of chironomids, midges and mayflies so a fly fisher must resort to tactics that can offer best results during non-hatch activity. If trout refuse to get frisky and come to the surface, then you have to go down to them. Fish the larva, nymph and emerging stages of the insects: bloodworm for the chironomid larva phase (see p. 88), mayfly nymph for the mayfly (p. 91–93), and midge and chironomid pupae for the latter's emerging periods (p. 83 and 89). The mature insects are anxious and restless, waiting for weather and ideal conditions to maximize their mating performances. Their pre-emergent activity is exciting for hungry trout.

Fishing Places

During May, low-elevation lakes that opened in mid-April, such as Dragon in Quesnel, are now in ideal spring condition: water temperature has warmed to above 10°C, plant life is once again in early stages of growth, leaves are in bud and water clarity has returned to normal after spring turnover. I'll fish Dragon faithfully while some of my other favourite local places are getting ready for the season: Opatcho, Tory, Vivian and Eena lakes and soon the Stellako River, which opens June 1.

Rivers flowing from large lakes that are open year-round to fishing, such as the Crooked, which courses north from Summit Lake above Prince George, are in terrific shape for clarity and bug life in May. They tend to be high from lake-spill of melting snow and perhaps cannot be waded easily, but are very productive right up to the banks using floating line, midge and mayfly dry patterns or small flashback pheasant nymphs. I wish we had more of them, those glistening, meandering and fruitful creeks and streams that are always open, which beckon the wandering angler to pursue their bounty, but sadly, the best river and stream trout season is still a few long months away.

Dragon Lake

You can never give up on Dragon—it's just too good a fishery and there is always the chance that you will tempt a 5-kg rainbow to take your

Brian Smith, Darcie Smith, BJ Bruder (née Smith) and dog Lugnut: early spring fishing on Dragon Lake. Dale Freschi photo.

offering. Although it has not been terrific to me and my buddies the past few seasons, we have caught some incredible fish to 5 kg, but recently not the double-digit numbers of large trout that we enjoyed five to ten years ago. Kevin Crawford, however, has done well, amassing many double-digit days of rainbows. Living on the lake and watching it daily for good fishing periods is an advantage few of us are afforded, and I can only speculate with deep jealousy about his good fortune in residing on a prime trout fishing lake.

May is a transition month for Dragon, featuring the awakening of the mass of insect life this trophy lake possesses. Chironomids, mayflies, scuds and leeches are the dominant hatches and staples provided to the fly fisher. If you go well armed with all of the April fly patterns I've shown you, plus mayfly nymphs and duns (hatching adults) both brown and olive, and the pupa and adult stage of small cinnamon caddis that often appears on Dragon during May, you should be rewarded with some trophy trout *if* you are lucky enough to hit it on the best days of the month.

Our annual Polar Coachman Flyfishers Fish-out takes place at Dragon in mid-May, a fun time where the catching is not as important as the fishing, the company is good and there's a noon barbecue. Some of the guys make a weekend out of it, but most of us just slide down from Prince George for the day, a quick ninety-minute run on paved roads.

Fly-fishing clubs are unique in their makeup. Some are very tight and protectionist, offering limited access for the beginner and emitting an almost snobbish air of importance. Others, like ours, are wide open to all walks of life, encouraging youth and family learning and participation, open fly-tying sessions and pleasant camaraderie that forms lifelong friendships. As many of us in the club enter our retirement years, our companionship and commitment to each other becomes deeper and envelops our personal lives, adding to the enrichment of our later years.

At the Fish-out in 2010, I was rewarded on my fifth cast of the day with a fine silver 60-cm plank of a trout on a little size #14 Mayfly Nymph Olive (see p. 91), my best fish of the young season. As it was, that beauty was my only fish of the day, and one of the few that were caught.

Opatcho Lake

In 2010 Opatcho opened late, in mid-April, and turned over by early May, signalling the opportunity to take a chance on tempting the large trout of this high-quality trophy lake. This is a lake that will seduce a fly fisher. It's small enough to cover in a day, has several weedy shoals and corners, and an abundance of insect life and moody but large fish—the perfect recipe for fly fishers who use small watercraft such as belly or pontoon boats and those who don't mind the occasional skunk while looking for a superior fishing experience.

My friends and good neighbours, Ken and Crystal Watson, have purchased the old fishing resort at Opatcho, which they have renovated and use as headquarters for the hunting/guiding business they operate. Ken has taken an interest in the fishery, convincing me that this is truly a special lake that needs to be figured out. As with all moody lakes, we know the trout are there; it's more a matter of persuading them to be a tad more cooperative.

After three May outings, once by myself, again with Dale Freschi and finally with Frank Vandenberghe, we thought we were getting a handle on Opatcho. We did not hit it hot, with any resemblance of a hatch during those three outings, but the dominant pattern colour that the trout ate was olive green: Carey, Bulldog, micro leech, chironomid and mayfly nymph. We also came across a few schools of chub minnows, which is disturbing news, because they are *not* supposed to be there and are not natural to our northern waters, usually being introduced by trollers using live-bait rigs. As a result, Frank also caught some nice fish using muddler minnow patterns, reasoning that the large Blackwater trout of Opatcho will feed on the live minnows—he was right, and they will.

If you fish Opatcho and use a fish finder, you will find the trout concentrated in 6–8 m of water and on the bottom. We found, however, trout that ventured to the shoals and weed beds during the day were fish actively searching for food; hence, could be caught. We released fish to 50 cm during our spring outings, which gave me the incentive to return to Opatcho in summer and fall with a glimmer of hope that it can produce limits of trophy trout.

Crooked River and Others

So many fly fishers beat themselves up trying to catch a lake at ice-off, clinging to a thread of hope they can "nail a trout every cast" once a lake opens for the season, that they overlook the real opportunity for terrific early-season trout fishing in our small river and creek systems.

Once buds have sprung on the cottonwoods and willows signalling that warm days are ahead, freshet will begin in earnest. Creeks and streams will be in flood, but until they are, water levels in small streams should remain high but clear—very fishable conditions. This window of opportunity lasts all through April in the north, and usually well into the last week of May. Early hatches of mayflies begin to appear, along with small stoneflies, midges, chironomids and often some early indications of caddis activity.

I confess to being one of the blissful ignorant, pounding our trout lakes in desperation on my too-seldom days off, frantically searching for that body of still water that will light up my winter slumber and arm wrestle me into spring fishing fever. What I should be doing is wandering the Crooked, Willow and Bowron rivers pursuing trout with a floating line and nymph, or perhaps a dry fly, which is my personal love and passion, when a hatch comes on in the early afternoon.

I plan to do more stream fishing this spring. I'll stroll and clamber the banks of our little waterways, poke around the corners, riffles and holes with a flashback pheasant or stonefly nymph, tempt some fickle trout with a silver bait-fish pattern and hopefully, when conditions are right, be rewarded with a hatch of early mayflies like the Blue-Winged Olive, or perhaps witness the spring emergence of early stoneflies.

Mayfly Patterns for Still Waters

Although still water in May is slowly warming to a trout's favourite temperatures of 12–15°C, this comfortable zone remains a month away—only a few low-elevation waters like Dragon have warmed to about 7–10°C, where you can expect prolific hatches of midge, chironomid, mayflies and perhaps little Cinnamon Caddis.

Successful patterns I showed you in April will surely turn the trick in May because many food organisms such as leeches, scuds and bloodworms are available year-round. However, expect to broaden your horizon with the increasing activity and emergence of more favourite trout foods: mayflies, both nymphs and adults; damselfly nymphs and the occasional caddis larva or emerging adult pupa.

Many fly fishers fish a chironomid through the entire season, but there is so much more to learn about the life cycle of a lake. For me, the true and meaningful beauty of fly fishing is the challenge of looking for and anticipating the "new" hatch, those glorious opportunities that present themselves to an observant angler every single month of the fly-fishing season. I may catch fewer fish than others but for me it's like being reborn to witness a new insect emerge, snip the chironomid from my leader early in the fishing year and chase the awakening insect hatch.

Mayfly Nymphs and Adults for Still Waters

Mayflies are the first new hatch to appear during May, causing trout to switch from chironomids and midges and gorge on these delicate little nymphs as they posture to begin the next stage of their life cycles. As a fly fisher, you must be observant—it's often the spotting of a solitary adult dun popping to the surface and drifting free on the lake that will signal to you that it's time to change lines and leaders.

The Callibaetis family of mayflies rules still water in the North Country. A much larger species than their river cousins, they are distinguished by their sailboat image, opaque wings upright to their bodies, drifting lazily on midday breezes. The hatching dun varies in body and wing colours from a muted cinnamon-brown with brown wings to grey-olive with smoky-grey wings.

Although always present in our lake and stream systems, mayfly nymphs are timid. They spend most of their aquatic life in hiding and don't get much attention from trout until they begin their restless pre-emergence activities during May. Nymphs feed on vegetation during their aquatic stage. Flora colour of a lake defines the colour of the insect—dominant green-bottomed waters produce olive nymphs, brown and dark-floored

Mayfly Adult Spinner. Brian Smith photo.

lakes generate brownish specimens. You can expect lakes like Dragon or Marmot to produce olive mayflies, tannin-rich still waters like Bishop or Rum Cache to create brown insects.

Unless there are large numbers of mayflies hatching, you are best to fish this emergent activity with a sinking line that will allow you to fish the bottom zone of the lake. If anchored in 3 m or less, consider a floating line with fluorocarbon leader and tippet that will sink rapidly and afford a long weed-free retrieve. From 3 to 5 m, think about a sink-tip or intermediate slow-sink line, and over 5 m, deploy a full-sink number 2 or 3 sink-rate line. During an intense adult dun hatch, your best action will usually be found in the upper metre of the zone, so work the area with a floating line and long leader that will allow you to switch to the adult if trout begin slashing the surface for drifting mayflies. There are lots of choices, but crazy action if you are lucky enough to be on the water for a strong emergence of mayflies.

Fish the nymph with a slow hand-twist retrieve, pausing often to let the imitation dangle and float freely in the mid-zone, frequently the trigger that will entice a trout to eat your fly. When fishing the adult dun, put it out there and leave it alone; allow the fly to drift on the breeze, which mimics the mature insect drying its wings before takeoff.

After hatching and becoming airborne, duns take to shoreline trees, where within a few days they transform into mature adult spinners, both male and female, and then return to the lake to mate and die. Spinners are recognized by their colouration: glossy charcoal-grey abdomens with pale ribbing, thoraxes almost black and transparent wings. Their two long double-body-length tails are a dominant feature, a beauty to behold during an intense mating spell, the swarms flitting and darting above the lake as if they were performing a symphony.

Sadly, their music is short-lived, for after they have mated and the females have deposited their eggs, both fall to the lake's surface, twitching but soon lifeless, thousands of them littering the water. Spinner falls create more dry-fly action for the fly fisher, trout always eager to annihilate egg-laying females as they drop to the surface to expend their seed, a little less interested in the dead spinners with wings spread after the ovipositing act.

Mayfly activity will last until August in northern lakes, the insects preferring calm cloudy days to bright sunshine, and cool weather to warm. Most activity begins around midday just when you are trying to eat your lunch, typical of most of my days on the water. I came to fish, not to eat, so I'll grab a bite on the run. As spring days wane to summer, mayfly emergences are less intense, the sizes of the adults diminish and trout search for upcoming new hatches: damselflies, caddis flies and dragonflies.

Mayfly Nymphs and Adults for Creeks and Rivers

You'll occasionally find large Callibaetis mayflies present in pools and backwaters of slow-moving streams, but in spring you are more likely to come across smaller early varieties of mayflies: the genus Baetidae, more commonly called the Blue-Winged Olive or BWO; or mayflies of the Trico family.

Although called "olives," BWOs are a multi-genus species and also present in colours of tan, black and pale grey. You can tie them in all of these colours if you wish, but I'm betting an olive as well as black replica will get you through all small mayfly-fishing situations, including the Trico hatch if you tie black patterns with pale wings down to size 22. You can never omit the venerable Adams patterns (see p. 95) from your fly box either, likely the most consistent hatch master of any mayfly ever invented—they are akin to the Woolly Worm or Doc Spratley wet flies for reliability.

During early spring on days that will not produce a hatch of may-flies, the most consistent patterns will surely be the nymph and emerger stages, well represented by the Flashback and Hare's Ear Nymphs plus Soft Hackle Emergers (see pp. 93–94) in sizes 14 to 18, fished dead drift in the current with floating line and 3-m leader tapered to 5-x tippet. This method is almost as gratifying as dry-fly fishing—no rise or splashy show, but next best because of light tippet and small fly patterns. If you are fishing slow, shallow waters with willow roots littering the bottom (like the Crooked River), a small strike indicator placed 1 m above your fly will save a lot of flies and tippet-tying exercises.

I must add that you can never go wrong fishing these three mayfly wet patterns on any river at any time of year—they are that deadly for any sulking fish during non-hatch activity.

Hope for June

In this part of British Columbia north of latitude 52, I often leave the month of May with a forlorn look on my fishing face, pondering what could have been, what should have been and ought to be; most years with that half-full feeling of eternal optimism. After all, there are probably only a handful of ideal solunar days during the month, which, combined with favourable weather conditions and a rising barometer, probably make for only five or six days in May that trout will feed voraciously and fishing will be terrific.

I think fly fishers often summarize our feelings with perpetual logic. If the fishing is poor, there are lots of excuses for it being so: weather, barometer, timing and poor guessing the most probable reasons.

Hurrah, June is next, one of the very best months of the year for multiple hatches, decent weather and predictable fishing opportunities.

June: An Explosion of Life

There is little that compares to the beauty of a northern June. It begins with the greening of our deciduous trees—birches, poplars, aspens, willows—and thickening undergrowth, and then the outburst of wildflowers—Indian paintbrushes, lupines, daisies and my personal favourite, wild roses.

Who cannot marvel and reflect on a good life when confronted with the rapturous fragrance of a stand of wild rose flowers? All the wild berry trees and shrubs spring into blossom: cranberries, saskatoon, gooseberries, currants, cranberries, mountain blueberries, huckleberries and raspberries, to name a few. It's a wonderful month to be alive and witness the beginning of another northern summer.

June can be a wet one, usually the wettest, interrupted almost daily with scattered thunderstorms that move rapidly through the region. They are, thankfully, short-lived and frantic. If you get caught in one, they often last only long enough to soak everything you own and water the wildflowers before blowing through to the next ridge. June is our third-warmest month, with daytime average high temperatures of 19°C, evening lows of 6°C. If a cold front moves in, as can often happen in June, hailstorms are frequent and our high-country lakes of the North Cariboo will be greeted with a late spring dump of snow.

A summer storm builds on Sheridan Lake in the Cariboo. Glenn Gerbrandt photo.

For the still-water fly fisher, it's one of the most reliable months of the year: hatches of chironomids, midges and mayflies are more consistent than in April and May; lake water is warming to near-perfect trout-seducing temperatures of 13–15°C; and the caressing winds no longer bite through your garments while you ply fertile northern still waters. An eager angler anticipates the beginning of the dry-fly season. The past winter is a blotted memory and the upcoming fall season is several months away.

Rivers and creeks are at their highest levels in June, swollen with snow-melt coming from high in their origins, augmented by heavy rains from frequent thunderstorms. These waterways are, however, teeming with insect life that has been waiting all spring for their chance at mating rituals. Stoneflies, midges, mayflies and caddis are beginning pre-emergence activity, restless and fidgety in their underwater worlds, anxious to become airborne.

Stoneflies are especially nervous as high-water periods are their ideal emergence times. This major hatch is often missed by the fly fisher who cannot get at the fish because of swollen rivers and difficult, if not treacherous, accesses.

Sometimes we get lucky and the snowpack is light and runoff is gradual. Rivers like the Blackwater (West Road) are in fishable condition opening day in the middle of June. The Stellako River, open to fishing June 1, is high but clear in June because it exits Francois Lake, has no tributaries and is only 11 km in length. Both can produce spectacular results fishing the early stonefly hatches.

Fishing Places

Of all the months of the year, June can be the best for the still-water fly fisher. In the Central Interior we are several weeks behind the Southern Interior's fishing season, but fertile low-altitude lakes of the North Cariboo can be at their peak during June. Forest, Elk, Dragon and Marmot lakes and all lakes in the North Cariboo below 1,000 m are in perfect shape for a fly-fishing expedition—not too warm to begin their summer doldrums periods, and not too cold to curtail the breeding and onslaught of insect hatches that will fatten worthy trout into the prime specimens we prize so dearly.

Mature trout that have been able to reproduce in tributary creeks of lakes, or those that entered false spawning stages where no spawning grounds exist, will be cleaning up, losing their dark colours and feeding voraciously. Once again they will be adversaries worthy of a fly fisher's attention.

As we move north to Central Interior lakes, major hatches of mayflies and chironomids continue in full swing, and will be active until late July. The water you fished in May will produce limits of prime trout, plus my favourite still waters around Prince George will be at their very best: Tory, Junkers, Opatcho, Hart, Vivian and Eena lakes, plus a myriad of lesser-known ponds and unnamed waters.

You can expect caddis to appear anytime in June, once deciduous leaves are fully open. Usually you'll only see the occasional one hatching during daylight hours, but once they begin to appear sporadically, hang around your favourite water until nightfall to witness their major emergence times.

June is also the beginning of damselfly season, not for fishing the adult insect but succulent (for a fish) nymphs that migrate from deep shoal water to shoreline reeds and vegetation to hatch into adults, which spend the summer mating and cruising the lakeshores. They are a pretty insect: males an electric blue; females olive-brown or grey-green. Their migration in the nymph stage is a major occurrence on all lakes and quiet streams, causing trout to target their midday movements. A trout's aggressiveness to this

Brian Nyberg with a "hog" rainbow over 65 cm long, typical of the biggest Hobson Lake trout. That's Cal Tant in the background. Glenn Gerbrandt photo.

hatch will bring ardent fly fishers to their knees with humble anticipation and forlorn glee.

River and stream fishing can be sporadic in June because of runoff and high-water conditions, but that doesn't mean there are no trout around. They are just more difficult to find and get to. Although rivers and streams often present difficult wading during June, I've had some of my best river and stream fishing occur in this month, especially the Crooked and on several occasions the Stellako and Blackwater rivers.

Life is good. June northern days are long, daylight lasting until past 10 p.m., morning arriving at 5 a.m.—lots of hours to fish your face off.

Tory Lake—Caddis Flies Anyone?

One of the smallest bodies of prime fly waters in the north, but also one of my favourites, Tory is regarded as one of my "home lakes," counted among those that are seldom unreliable and regularly offer consistent and predictable hatches. The average trout in the lake measures 40–45 cm, but I am sometimes awarded one over 50 cm, a respectable size in any fly fisher's diary.

June fishing at Tory can be summarized in one word: anticipation. It's the expectation of a day that trout will venture onto the abundant shoals to feed, and of their willingness to rise and eat dry flies. These are fine attributes for any fishery regardless of trout size, and features that make Tory a quality fishery.

Tory Lake is accessed from the Blackwater Road, which runs south from Hwy 16 West within Prince George city limits. Take the Pelican Forest Service Road (FSR) at about the 25-km point, which reaches southwest into the Batnuni country. Tory is at km 43 of the Pelican FSR. The lake has a Forest Service campsite with pit toilet and room for three units. There is no boat launch but, with a steep hill to navigate with your watercraft, water access is best served with a float tube or pontoon boat.

In 2009, I fished Tory in mid-April with friend Frank Vandenberghe the day after ice-off, then again in May by myself and in June on two occasions. April and May results were disappointing but average by fishing standards, picking up five to eight trout per trip, fishing with a dependable early spring leech pattern, the Olive Seal Bugger.

June was another story! My pal Bob Graham and I were there June 10, a beautiful day with rising barometer and temperature in the high teens, both prime conditions for the season's first hatches of either caddis or damsels, or perhaps if we were fortunate, both insect species.

Caddis flies are my favourite adult insect searching patterns. Trout relish them, and will look for them through the entire summer. I learned something about them this past fishing season. Because trout love to eat them, you can *create* a caddis hatch, and if trout are rising to insects of *any* species, they will rarely refuse a well-presented caddis.

We fared well. Bob and I released many nice trout on that June day, most in the 40-cm range, a few over 45 cm, mine all on the surface with Mikulak Traveler Caddis #12 (see p. 97).

Father's Day, June 20, was another "Tory" day. Joining Dale Freschi and me were my two daughters Brianna (BJ) and Darcie, both in their early twenties and wanting to spend the day fishing with their daddy on his special day, and very special it was. Dale and I released about fifty on caddis fly imitations, me once more on the Mikulak Traveler, Dale on floating line and olive caddis pupa. We fished in belly or pontoon boats. The girls fared well also, picking up several nice trout.

My most memorable family moment of the day came at lunchtime, the girls and I celebrating our occasion with cigars, Dale chuckling at the sight of the three of us smoking it up while fish were on the bite.

Boundary Lake—More Caddis!

Boundary is a pretty little lake on the north side of Prince George, lying in the foothills of the Rocky Mountains. It's reached by turning east on the North Fraser Road, which leaves Hwy 97 North about 30 km north of Prince George. Travel east on gravel for about 23 km and then north up the Averill Road about 5 km.

The Forest Service campsite at Boundary offers a car-top launch, pit toilets, room for three to four camping units, and is accessible for small motorhomes and trailers, truck and camper or tenting parties. One feature I noticed about Boundary is the lack of beetle kill sign in the area, the lake being attended by mainly fir and spruce forest, a real treat after seeing millions of acres of Blackwater Road forest consumed by the vicious beetle over the past fifteen years.

On June 26 my friend Bob Graham invited me to share one of his fishing spots. It was my first time there and I was joined by another good friend, Kevin Beatty. Kevin and I bounced along the rough North Fraser Road for at least a half-hour after missing the turnoff, turned back after we spotted an elk running up the road in front of us at km 43 (must have been an omen), and almost drove by the darn junction again on the way back. It's a good thing I had to get out for a pee and noticed the well-hidden North Averill sign or I'm certain we would still be looking for Boundary Lake.

The trout at Boundary are on the small side for our country, averaging 30–35 cm. Feisty as hell in spite of their size, many trout were more than willing to be seduced by the dry fly, again rising consistently to the Mikulak Caddis Traveler (see p. 97) without any visible signs of a hatch.

My friends are still shaking their heads. During my last three outings, I have fished only my Mikulak dry, and have caught and released over a hundred trout not counting the misses, which are few on caddis because they take them with such joyful force. I know Bob Graham was converted that day on Boundary, as he told me he had several good outings on the caddis dry after that. You don't need a hatch to fish a caddis—proven!

Stellako River—Even More Caddis!

Even if the Stellako is a tough fishing place, reluctant to give up secrets, it's arguably still one of the world's best trout rivers. It's one of the best because the river's trout are a wild strain, its hatches are prolific and numerous and the rainbows fickle; but mostly, it's a learning place for any angler who wishes to become a better fly fisher.

To fish the Stellako, think smaller than when you consider lakes: small flies, light tackle, fine tippets and long leaders. Most hatches, except stoneflies and drakes, are of small to diminutive varieties, sizes #14 down to #20 in all insect species: caddis flies, mayflies and midges. I know about the "red apple theory"—throw your biggest and brightest fly at them—but it rarely works in the Stellako, especially in the bridge runs in the top part of the river. These bridge-dwelling trout, even the 25-cm two-year-olds, see thousands of flies each year, and know the difference between correct size, colour and attractors.

Stellako trout are also perceptive to "drag," the curse of the beginning river fisher that only practice, many refusals and then results from learning better casting techniques will overcome. The student learns that controlling line "drag" is mandatory, keeping casts short, the leader long and fine and fly line mended upstream of the floating fly. You learn to practise position more than distance, technique and quality of casts more than quantity.

The river teaches you to wade softly, break runs and currents into workable sections, and cover both sides of its seams with quick, short casts and high, floating patterns. Work upstream whenever possible, from the bottom of runs upward, but throw downstream parachute casts at large trout when you can sight them, showing the fly to the fish before the leader. Remember that river trout face upstream into the current, are oblivious to minor commotion below them but can see you in their window of vision when fishing from above them.

Like all fishing waters, the Stellako has its moods and best times. First light is always good for a few large trout, especially on small flashbacks or large stonefly nymphs; midday has expectations of mayfly and midge hatches; evenings after supper feature caddis and the return of egg-laying midges and mayflies.

The Stellako fishes well in June if water levels are below normal and early spring weather warms it enough to bring on the season's first strong hatches. Like all trout fishing, it's a crap shoot, but a worthy one if you catch it right.

On a spring camping trip west with Bob Graham, we detoured to the Stellako on June 17 for a few days, looking for scrapping rainbows and a hope that we could find them receptive to the dry fly. The water temperature of the river at the Glenannan Bridge outflow from Francois Lake was a "balmy" 10°C, too frigid for swimming, but warm enough to produce the first caddis hatches of the young season.

We fished only one evening, but it was a glorious one. The Stellako was up to its old tricks again, offering simultaneous multiple hatches that can leave a fly fisher scratching his head, pulling hair and flogging the water in bewildered solitude. We began clobbering trout on the Spotted Caddis #14 (see p. 101) about 8 p.m., and I promptly took eight nice 35–45-cm fish on successive casts, then nothing doing. Daylight was fading and they flipped to the other three egg-laying insects that were peppering the water: rusty spinners, Blue-Winged Olives and that curse of all fly fishers, size #22 grey Tricos.

I wish I could say we figured it out and became heroes (in our minds), but no, it was not to be as we beat the river with perfect casts until darkness with nary a pull, trout rising around our waders as twilight became nightfall.

Dusk at Tezzeron Lake. ·
Erich Franz photo.

Frustrated? Heck no, just curious. As I pondered the outing in my sleeping bag after the event, I reasoned the only thing I didn't do was go wet. If I had fished a soft hackle nymph size #18 or so, it would have worked... I think. And that's why I love the Stellako River.

Junkers Lake—A Northern Gem

Wild trout, breathtaking scenery and good company—what more can you ask for from a day on Junkers? The native trout come from a long line of progeny established during the last ice age ten thousand years ago that left the North Country sprinkled with large and small lakes, equally great rivers and little creeks and streams, all connected and favourable to the creation of a fishery that is remote and self-supporting.

The fact that these waterways are the beginnings of the Arctic watershed that flows to the Peace River and eventually the Mackenzie River to the Arctic Ocean is truly mind-boggling—as the crow flies, over 3,000 km of isolated wilderness and water originating from humble beginnings in northern British Columbia (and Alberta).

Junkers is accessed by pickup truck or 4x4 from Hwy 97 north of Prince George. Turn east on the Firth Lake Forest Service (FS) Road about forty km north of Bear Lake, staying on this main road for about twenty minutes' driving time to the lake. The access road to the lake is steep but passable with 4x4 vehicles, but don't expect to launch a boat carried with trailer because the lake access has no turnaround capability—it's ideally a canoe, float tube or pontoon boat type of lake. I've seen fishermen carry their boats, motors and gear down the hill, but it's a lot of work for a few fish.

The scenery around Junkers is as good as it gets in the north, especially later in the year when the leaves are turning: steep, rolling terrain in the Rocky Mountain Trench; spruce and deciduous forest teaming with big game; and roadsides abounding with spring wildflowers. It's a secluded and blissful experience that any outdoors person will truly appreciate.

June 6 is usually a bit early for a Junkers expedition, but Dale Freschi and I were eager to give it a try because of the early spring thaw of 2010. In spite of Dragon Lake being ice-free on March 29, the Interior Plateau north of Prince George is less forgiving: higher elevation, colder, heavier snowfalls and ice-off usually three to four weeks behind the North Cariboo and Nazko–Blackwater country lakes.

I like to target Junkers in late June and July, hoping for caddis and damselfly hatches, and again in early October a few weeks before freeze-up, fishing leeches and dragonfly nymph patterns. Chironomid fishing is the way to go in May or early June, working the shelves at the south and

Sunrise at Tezzeron Lake. Erich Franz photo.

north ends and the long ledge and deep transition hole in the middle neck of the lake.

On June 6 the winds were low but from the north; always a poor barometer indicator in my fishing experience, but never a reason to not go fishing. The trout were pouting, lying in 8 m of water with zipper mouths—usually a recipe to go deep with attractors like Bulldogs (see p. 87) or Muddlers (see p. 84) and tease them out of their bad moods.

When trout are uninterested and unwilling to participate, we have found that you need to rile them, appealing to their aggressive nature by fast-stripping large patterns through their holding places, forcing them into aggressive action. It often works, and that day it did—we had a lot of short bumps, but connected with several trout over 50 cm and many in the 45-cm range, average size for Junkers.

Junkers is not a protected fishery, so it's an angler's duty to look after what regulations fail to address. To me, it makes no sense to kill a limit of large, wild trout in a fragile environment that has no stocking program to sustain its numbers. We have witnessed too many people killing wild trout at places like Junkers, a shame for the resource. Take one home for the barbecue. They are great-tasting fish, but please remember it took five years of natural growth in a harsh situation for your trophy trout to gain its prominence as a lunker, and only a moment to end its life with a bonker.

Crooked River—I Return

Spring 2011 was a dismal write-off: wet weather, high water and blustery winds that delayed the fishing season by at least two weeks. Hatches were sporadic during the month of May, but improved as June approached.

I promised myself I would spend more time in the little Crooked during May, but record-high snowbanks still gripped the river for all of April and well into May, keeping me from tackling the willow-infested banks to sample the early spring fishery that I know exists on the Crooked.

When you get those perfect days in early spring—rising barometer, water warming to mid-teens Celsius, bugs hatching and air temperatures approaching 20°C—you need three things to make your fishing life tolerable: time from work, bug repellent and a 3-weight fly rod in hand.

In the Crooked River's life, everything happens earlier because of its origins at Summit Lake, warm water springs and its unwillingness to completely freeze during winter. Insect hatches come to life two to three weeks earlier than other streams in the region and water levels from spring runoff peak by the end of May, dropping the river into prime conditions for the month of June.

In mid-June 2011, even allowing for a late spring, the Crooked finally came into its own and was teeming with insect hatches, the eager trout splurging on the available bounty of its fertile waters. It's a good time for the trout, the mature rainbows having spawned and looking for food to replenish their strength, the immature ones keenly rising in every corner pool and riffle to eat every insect offering presented.

On that perfect day, hatches were overlapping: stoneflies, both little olives and big skwalas; mayflies—Tricos, green drakes and flavinas; and small Spotted Caddis flies. Wanting to fish small patterns and knowing a trout's fondness for eating green drakes, I wisely chose a green drake size #14 parachute style, and proceeded to catch and release many fine rainbows in but four hours of fishing, enjoying my finest-ever day on the Crooked.

As I hiked back to the truck and put my fly rod away for the day, I reflected on the experience, realizing that the day had been special and may never come to me again... and that is why we call it "fishing."

June Fly Patterns for Still Waters

June signals insect activity for the largest lake-dwelling insects: caddis flies, damselflies and the biggest specimens of interest to fly fisher (and fish)—dragonflies. All of them are active, hatching and breeding through the northern summer months of June, July and August.

For the fly fisher who loves to fish the surface (like me), trout commonly snub their noses at midge and chironomid hatches, refusing to expend the effort to rise. I think, in the trout's mind, this is mostly because of safety. Why expose yourself for little bugs when you can gorge in comfort on millions of midge and chironomid larvae and pupae staging on a shoal below the surface? When the big boys (and girls) of summer begin to frolic, however, it's a different attitude for fish—this is their time, a chance to fatten up with meals that are up to fifty times more protein-bearing than their normal table fare. If I were a trout, and my wife often remarks that I think like one (whatever that means), I would be anxious for summer fun. Wouldn't you?

The stage for the big insect show is set in June, actors and support crew in place. The movie begins: fly fishers laden with old and new fly patterns, favourite fly rods, good company and comfortable equipment. Weather and barometer are favourable, wind calm, and trout eager. All adversaries pray in their own way: fly fishers that the "fish god" will smile on them once more, that their fly patterns will be accepted and their lines will straighten with fine fish. Trout must surely hope for a quick release; failing that, compassion and a swift death for their errors in judgment. It's a good movie—for the fly fisher, one played many times over the past winter. All that's missing on summer water is the popcorn maker.

Caddis Fly: Larva, Pupa and Adult

Trout rising to the dry fly with abandonment and vigour—in lake or river, nothing can spur this action better than a caddis hatch. As a precursor to this adult activity, there are several weeks of opportunity available to the fly fisher using larva and pupa stages of caddis flies, which are also large meal-ticket items for foraging trout during non-hatch periods of insect movement.

Caddis flies' larvae develop from eggs laid by adults the previous summer, living in encased solitude by building houses around themselves with sticks, small pebbles and bottom debris collected and glued together from their expended secretions.

Larvae cases resemble discarded cigar butts or slender unruly gobs of weeds. As they develop they need to rebuild the homes they have outgrown, often several times before they are mature enough to pupate. When they leave their cases to search for new home-building materials larvae are perfect targets for fish—juicy, unprotected morsels as they crawl along the bottom of lakes and ponds looking for fodder to rebuild their dwellings.

In soft bottoms of clear still-water lakes, you'll often see trails that wandering larvae have left behind, small meandering trenches resembling dugout paths from a miniature grub hoe. This is the ideal time of year to use Woolly Worm patterns (see p. 96), rough hairy-looking flies that are best fished very slowly, crawling your offerings through the bottom zones of lakes with type 3 sinking fly lines. You'll often snag your flies on bottom debris, but more often than not hook up with a prime fighting trout that cannot resist the tender delicacy of big caddis larvae. Woolly Worms are excellent choices for the trolling fly fisher as long as you fish them deeply and slowly; drifting your boat, propelled only by the wind, unafraid of the occasional bump on the bottom or weed hookups.

Caddis larvae vary in colour: dark-bottomed lakes will produce tan-coloured insects, whereas clear algae-type water will generate pale or dark olive larvae species, their colouration tending to adapt to vegetation sources they feed upon. Keep this in mind when choosing your patterns.

Preceding early mayfly hatches during the month of May, caddis fly larvae begin to undergo a metamorphosis. They have been maturing all spring, outgrowing and rebuilding their encasements. Finally, they seal their cases and begin the third stage of their development into pupae that become adult-resembling insects within their enclosures. They also form two oar-like appendages. When ready to migrate, pupae leave their cases and swim using these paddles, which help propel them quickly to the surface to avoid being targeted by bottom-cruising fish.

As they near the surface, pupae often travel great distances just under the surface film as they struggle to split their cases. When free of its case, the adult caddis emerges and lifts its wings to dry. Once that is accomplished, the insect skitters and runs across the top water in its effort to become airborne and free itself from foraging trout.

Caddis pupae look similar to dragonfly nymphs; pupae, however, are a couple of sizes smaller and lack tail filaments. Another difference is that sedge pupae hatch *in* the lake, visible insect shucks you observe floating on the surface during or after the hatch activity of the previous evening. Dragonfly nymphs have no pupa stage and crawl to shore or some kind of structure to hatch, leaving their shucks on rocks, logs or shoreline rushes.

Most often, caddis pupae are olive-toned but can be found in other colours or multi-coloured (my preference): Naples yellow (yellow-gold) with bright green rib and cinnamon thorax; muted grey with green rib and

A lucky trout gets her freedom at Sheridan Lake in the Cariboo.
Glenn Gerbrandt photo.

bright green thorax; cinnamon with yellow or green rib and bright green thorax.

You should fish pupae imitations with a fly line and sinking leader that will allow you the time to slowly work through shoal water 3 m deep and shallow water of less than 1 m. Depending on surface activity, the most effective lines are type 2 sink tips, intermediate full sink, hover and floating. I like to target the pupae migration in less than 2 m of water with a floater, which can quickly become versatile to fish the Mikulak adult (see p. 97) when trout are slashing the surface feeding on recently hatched wing-drying caddis flies.

Another option—my preferred one when fishing in my punt boat— is to set up two fly rods: one a soft 4-weight rod with floating line, 3-m nylon copolymer leader and Mikulak sedge (see p. 97); the other a 4- or 5-weight medium-action rod armed with a Rio Versa-tip and selection of Airflo Polyleaders, available in seven different sink rates. I used to own two mid-priced reels of the same model and seven interchangeable spools with fly lines of varying sink rates. I now own two very expensive reels with two versa-tip lines, but can change the leader set-up in a minute to accommodate different sink-rate preferences.

Of all lake hatches, adult caddis flies are the most fun to fish and the ones I reminisce about during our long northern winters. You probably get tired of me writing about it, but my dreams are infested by the sight of my Mikulaks being ripped off the surface by 1- or 2-kg trout. If you haven't done so, you owe yourself a favour to put chironomids aside and dedicate some time for fishing adult caddis flies on any summer day in June, July, August or September. If fish are rising, they will eat it—I guarantee it. If they are not rising, they will still take it. It'll only take one; you'll be hooked and your spouse will wonder what you're really dreaming about.

Fish the adult caddis with a long soft leader, floating line and lots of patience. When trout rise around you, quickly throw it in their rings and let it sit for a minute. If it doesn't bring a strike, lift your rod and skitter the fly a few metres, imitating a hatching caddis. If the trout refuses, it may have turned in another direction. If you weren't watching the rise to see which direction the trout was heading, take an educated guess on its course, redirect your cast 3 m to either side of the first rise and repeat the process. I've had trout rise 1 m from the boat and splash me in the face while taking caddis flies.

If trout are not rising, anchor off a shoal in deep water on the transition shelf and cast well onto the shoal. Work your fly into deep water, trying to coax wary fish lying off the shallows in deep water to eat your offering. Most caddis flies hatch in less than 2 m of water, but trout are cautious about venturing onto shallow shoals on bright sunny days—they will, however, linger off the shelf in anticipation of a vagrant insect coming their way. Game on.

Damselfly Nymph

All fly fishers worthy of their vises welcome the June migrations and emergences of much-extolled damselfly adults, which are missing one day and then suddenly appear in swarms on still-water lakes in Interior BC regions. They signal that the damselfly's journey from shelf-water nymph to beautiful and delicate adult has begun.

Experienced fly fishers crave this hatch, often targeting their two-week fishing sojourns into the Interior around the upcoming damsel migration, their thoughts and fishing dreams focused on finding perfect timing and ripe conditions for this major event.

Damselfly adults are recognized by their likeness to their close cousins, the big dragonflies. At first glance they can be mistaken for the larger insect, but there are many differences: damsels have long slender bodies, dragonflies are long-bodied but robust; damsels fold their wings over their backs at rest, dragonflies hold theirs perpendicular to their bodies; dragonflies are about twice the size and length of damselflies. Colourations of both insects are similar: bright blue with black bands for boys, drab olive and browns for girls.

If you are visiting a lake you have never fished before and wonder whether you will have damselfly expectations, first look at the vegetation and then the shoreline for ideal damselfly habitat. Abundant plant growth, like lush Chara weed and algae, indicates that the water has the high pH that is conducive to damselfly production. If your prospect lake is tannin-coloured and lacking thick weed beds, it's unlikely that it has proper calcium minerals for good creation of crustacean or insect skeletons.

Another indicator is the shoreline. If it lacks grasses, bulrushes or long-stemmed lily pads for damsel nymphs to crawl up on to hatch, it's unlikely you will be hunting fish in key damsel country with damselfly patterns.

Damselflies develop from eggs laid by adults, the larva or nymph stage being the most important to the fly tier and fisher. Eggs develop and transform quickly into minute nymphs that go through several moults, taking one to two years to mature and prepare themselves for migration and adulthood. They are always available to fish, but live in seclusion in the weed growth, rarely venturing out of their watery hideaways.

When conditions are right, however (water temperature, lunar cycle, and barometer), the signal comes and off they go in mass migration from shelf water to shoals, rising to the subsurface and swimming slowly and lazily into the next blue yonder of their fragile lives. Once they have located a firm footing on a weed stem (or even a fisher's boat or belly boater's net) it takes only a minute for them to dry their skeletons, split their cases and transform into the graceful flying insects that we know as damselflies.

Trout will occasionally key on adults, but not often. You are more likely to find this happening at the end of the several-weeks' migration cycle after they have seen many nymphs, had their fill of them and are still feeling frisky about damselflies. Migrating nymphs are prime targets for trophy trout, food they can gather without the risk of exposure to all of the bad things that can happen to them on the surface: eagles, ospreys and those pesky, lurking fly fishers.

Fish migrating nymphs with a floating line in water less than 2 m deep. Use intermediate or short 2-m number 2 sinking-tip fly lines in water greater than 2 m. Nymphs will be migrating from deep to shallow water searching for shoreline reeds, swimming with undulating motions in the lake's upper zone. This movement can be well represented by a slow hand-crawl retrieve method interspersed with short resting periods. The fly's take is a violent, slashing motion as competitive trout charge from the depths to intercept exposed tender morsels. You will rarely miss a strike or get short hits from trout when fishing a damsel nymph.

Sight fishing is common when fishing damsel nymphs. Trout will cruise shallow littoral zones, often knocking nymphs off reeds as they clamber up stalks to find their coming-out places. All this makes for spectacular memories that will be etched in the minds of fly fishers, providing fine fodder for campfire reminiscences for many years to come. Lucky you.

Dragonfly Nymph

Last, but certainly not least in the fly fisher's array of worthy insect patterns for June and the upcoming months is the largest morsel of the year for foraging still-water trout—the princely dragonfly nymph. Always present in the trout's environment but preferring to be well hidden and solitary, dragonfly nymphs occupy drop-off areas of the lakes we fish, so are a good choice for a searching pattern during periods of little activity, or to find action on a lake that we don't know very well. All lakes and ponds have them; they are at the top of the food chain in their environments.

Like their cousins the damselflies, dragonflies develop through three stages: egg, larva or nymph and adult. Unlike damselflies, dragons take up to four years to mature, moulting through as many as a dozen instar stages that can preoccupy them through most of the summer fishing season. After instars, for a short period of a week or so, nymphs are soft-shelled and pale-coloured as their skeletons develop and darken into their normal camouflage colours of ruddy olive-green and grey tones.

In our waters, dragonfly nymphs are found in two key families: darners and red-shouldered (see pp. 100–101). Darners, larger and more mobile than red-shouldered nymphs, hunt their prey (damsel and mayfly nymphs, scuds and water boatmen) by chasing them down; red-shouldered prefer to lie in wait to intercept their quarry. Darner imitations are better searching patterns, but both are good fish catchers when the insects are migrating.

Adult darners are larger than the red-shouldered family and are long and slender with colouration much like damselflies—bright blue, banded with black or drab olive tones banded with black or brown. Red-shouldered adults are robust and squat in appearance, also sporting olive and grey-toned colourations.

Mature dragonfly nymphs, like damselflies, migrate shoreward from shelf water to complete their metamorphosis to adulthood. Like river-dwelling stonefly nymphs, dragonflies crawl to shore along the bottom of the lake, most often under cover of darkness or during the twilight period of summer days, making this insect a prime but often neglected selection for evening and early morning fishing.

Dragonfly nymphs are fished on the bottom, almost always with deep sinking #3–6 lines or sink tips, because that is where they hang out, chasing their food sources around in the weeds. There are occasions, when fishing long, shallow, weedy shoals, that you should consider a floating line and lead-weighted pattern, dragging your offering through these areas. During the prime migration months of June and July, anchor well up onto a likely weed flat facing the drop-off and fish your patterns onto the shelf from the bottom zone with a slow hand-crawl retrieve, imitating migrating and travelling nymphs.

Fly Patterns for Open-water Months

March
Stonefly Patterns

Stonefly Nymph, Little Brown

Originator: unknown (tied & modified by Brian Smith 2004)
Hook: Tiemco 200R #16
Thread: UTC, grey-olive
Underbody: lead wire, .015; 6–8 turns under front thorax portion
Tails (2): boar bristles, black; tied both sides of a ball of goose primary barbs
Rib: copper wire, fine; 4–5 turns counter-wound over abdomen
Abdomen: Canada goose primary barbs, dark grey
Wing case pads (2) and thorax pad (1): dark turkey primary section
Thorax: peacock herls
Throat hackle: grouse feather, dark phase
Tying tips: This pattern is tied similar to all of my stonefly imitations, just in smaller sizes. The trick in keeping the tail fibres separated is to begin by tying a ball of abdomen material (whether primary or dubbing) at the bend of the hook.

Wing pad design on stonefly patterns can also be difficult to grasp. Begin by binding a 5-mm width turkey section on top of the hook shank at about the halfway point, points to the rear. Lash in peacock herl thorax material and take 2 turns of herl in front of the turkey section. Tie the herl off, bring the turkey section over the top, fasten it with 3 turns of thread, fold the turkey back on itself and tie down again, creating a pad effect. Repeat this procedure for the second wing pad. Finally, after the last thorax herl procedure, attach the throat hackle, and bring the last turkey segment forward over the thorax and finish the head.

Stonefly Adult, Little Brown

Originator: unknown (tied & modified by Brian Smith 2004)
Hook: Tiemco 2312 #14–18
Tail: elk hairs 10–12 stacked, ½ body length
Body: floss, black, single strand

Wing: elk hairs, body & tail length

Feelers: boar bristles, black; 1 each side of eye

Hackles (2): grizzly & brown, 3 turns each

Tying tips: To keep the bulk down and prevent tying lumps in the body, I begin this pattern by tying the tail material at the ¾-point of the shank, winding thread over the tail fibres all the way to the bend of the hook. Take 2 turns of thread under the tail to "set" the fibres above the shank, and then wind the thread back to the tail tie-in point. The body floss is attached at this ¾ point, spiralled down to the tail and returned to the tie-in point, which forms a smooth and tidy transition for the fly.

Dry-fly hackles are always attached tip forward and concave (cupped or flat) side toward the eye of the hook, which aids in floatation of the pattern, then trimmed to the gap of the hook by cutting a slim "V" along the underside of the hackles, which assists the fly to ride upright and level on the water. I treat all of my dry flies with silicone boot spray like Pro-Tex brand, which is colourless and aids the fly's ability to shed water and shake dry after wetting.

Another tip: if you are looking for boar bristles, you will find them on any pure bristle paint brush.

Midge Patterns

Midge Larva

Originator: unknown (tied & modified by Brian Smith 2008)

Hook: Tiemco 200R #16–18

Thread: UTC, red

Tail: marabou, red; clipped short

Underbody: UTC threads, red

Body: Larva Lace, red

Hackle: pheasant, small reddish back feather; body and tail length, only a few barbs

Head: ostrich, grey; only a few turns

Tying tips: The appearance of translucence and segmentation of a larva's body is our goal when tying this pattern, achieved by the use of Larva Lace wrapped forward from the tail. To keep the body material from looking "lumpy" at the tie-in point, trim the lace to a fine point before tying it in at its very tip, and then stretch the lace when wrapping it up the shank.

I've discovered a little trick with hackle that should help you put just a few barbs on the hook. Using a small back feather with reddish tones, trim the fuzz, pull the barbs back, cut out the tip section forming a "V" and then pluck the remaining to only a few barbs. Lay the section on top of the hook—concave side down—at the "V" separating the barbs and bind it down with only 2 turns of thread. Once completed, give the feather-base a good twist to lay the barbs flat along the shank, sweeping backward. This gimmick can be used on any pattern that requires a hint of hackle that circles the shank.

Midge Pupa

Originator: unknown (modified & tied by Brian Smith 2001)
Hook: Tiemco 2487 #16–20
Thread: UTC, black
Tail: none
Rib: silver wire, extra fine
Abdomen: goose primary barbs, grey
Gills: Glo Yarn white; posted at the eye, trimmed short
Thorax: peacock herl, 2 turns
Tying tip: I like to tie in the Glo Yarn after the abdomen and before the thorax, and then use the herl to cover the rest of the thorax area.

Wing cases on models of the pupae stage, although present, can be omitted from the pattern because of the very small size of midge imitations. I do include them when tying my chaoborus pupa model, however, because this replica has no gill representation.

Midge Adult Emerger

Originator: Brian Smith 1993
Hook: Mustad 94840 #16–22
Thread: UTC, grey
Tail (shuck): deer-hair fibres, natural grey, body length
Back: deer hair, natural grey; tied as shell back over body
Body: goose primary barbs (2), natural grey
Hackle: grizzly saddle; 3 turns

Tying tips: For alternative body colours, use olive green goose primary barbs or cock pheasant sword barbs in cinnamon brown. Begin by tying a 3-mm wide section of deer hair for the tail shuck at the ⅔-shank point, wrap it down the shank to the bend and tie off. Tie the next 3-mm section of deer hair for its back *by the tips* at the bend, then the body primary can be tied and brought forward. Finally, the back is wrapped over the body and hackle is the last step.

Minnow Patterns for Coastal Rivers

Egg-n-Eye (Kitimat River style)

Originator: unknown (tied & modified by Brian Smith)
Hook: Tiemco 9394 #6–8
Thread: UTC, black
Tail: mallard flank, natural; ½ body length, 5-cm strip folded
Body: Mylar silver, counter-wound with silver wire (for strength)
Underwing: Fish-Fuzz, brown; sparse, body & tail length
Overwing: Crystal Hair, blue or pearl; body & tail length
Throat: Glo-Yarn Sockeye Red; clipped short
Tying tips: This pattern originated in the 1960s, first tied with mallard overwing and without flash. With the advent of modern materials, the pattern has become an attractor as well as a food item for trout—they find it hard to pass up.

A tip for this and any Mylar body: tie in the tail and silver wire first, beginning 2 cm behind the eye of the hook; take both the tail and wire to the bend of the hook. Return to the tie-in point. For Mylar, first trim the strip to a fine point; tie in by the point at the 2-cm spot, then wrap down and *back up* the shank to the tie-in point.

A tip for any flash material: take 3 strands about 10-cm long (for size #8 hook); tie one half-length on top to the far side of your hook, and then bend the remainder back toward you and tie it on the close side of the hook—trim all to the same length.

Murray's Rolled Muddler (with added flash)

Originator: Tom Murray, Vancouver, BC, 1960s (tied & modified by Brian Smith)
Hook: Tiemco 9394 #6–10

Thread: UTC, red
Tail: mallard flank, ½ body length, 5-cm strip folded
Body: Mylar silver; counter-wound with silver wire (for strength)
Wing: mallard, natural; 10-cm strip folded twice lengthwise, body & tail length
Overwing: Polar Flash, pearl; body & tail length
Head: pale deer hair; spun, clipped bullet-shaped, flattened on the bottom; leave a few strands trailing to rear over wings
Tying tips: Leave room for the deer hair by beginning the tie-in at the ¾-shank point of hook. When tying this pattern, to make it effective you need to show at least 5 cm of red tying thread on the shank *under* the wings and bullet head.

April
Scud (Freshwater) Shrimp

Gammarus Shrimp

Originator: unknown (modified & tied by Brian Smith)
Hook: Tiemco 2457 #8–16
Thread: UTC, olive green
Underbody: lead wire .020 (or width of hook wire) in the middle of the shank, over-wrapped with a few strands of olive embroidery thread to "fatten" the midriff
Tail: olive-dyed mallard flank, sweeping well below the bend of hook
Shellback: Midge Flex, ¼ inch, olive
Body: dubbing, Chan's Stillwater Soft Blend olive
Hackle: brown saddle, palmered 6–7 turns over dubbing
Rib: gold wire, fine; 6–7 turns over shellback and body
Tying tips: If you tie everything onto the hook in the order I have listed, you shouldn't have trouble with this scud pattern—one hint is to leave a little extra room at the head because you are tying off four items in the same spot, which can tend to cause bulk. Alternative dubbing colours that I use for shrimp are Borden's Hare-Tron HT10 Golden Stone, Scintilla Dub SD17 Sooty Olive, Hare-Tron #24 Olive, and a pale chartreuse green that you'll never find; it was

given to me as a ball of Phentex material by Jack Shaw in the 1970s; I chop it up and make dubbing from it, and I have a lifetime supply.

Hyalella Shrimp

Originator: unknown (modified & tied by Brian Smith)
Hook: Tiemco 2457 #14–18
Thread: UTC, watery olive
Tail: mallard barbules, olive; only a wisp of a tail
Shellback: Midge Flex, clear ¼ inch; tied over body
Body: dubbing, colour Ligas 42 Sparkle Olive Scud
Legs: body dubbing, picked out with dubbing needle

Leech Patterns

Leech, Blood Bugger

Originator: Brian Smith 1993
Hook: Mustad 9671 #8–14
Thread: UTC, black
Underbody: lead wire .015–.025 mm; 10–12 turns on front half of hook shank
Tail: marabou, black; tips only, tied body length
Hackle: black saddle; 1½ times hook gap, palmered through body
Body: dubbing, Arizona Simi Seal, colour Bloody Leech
Tying tips: Any time I am wrapping tail material, I like to begin binding it at about ¾-shank length of the hook and follow it with thread to the hook bend—if you learn to do this with all of your tails, you will eliminate bulk knots at the bend of your hook, which is very important when tying smooth bodies. You'll have better-looking flies if you repeat the habit for all of your patterns.

For leech patterns, begin to bind the tail after the lead wire ends at about ½-shank length. Tie in the saddle hackle, next the body, and then spiral the hackle over the body to the head. Your leech patterns will look better if you rough them up with a dubbing teaser after the hackle has been applied—it evens the dubbing and pulls the hackle rearward into the body.

Leech, Micro Bead Head

Originator: unknown (tied by Brian Smith)
Hook: Mustad 9671 #12–14
Head: gold bead
Tail: marabou, black; tips only, tied body length
Body: Arizona Simi Seal, colour Bloody Leech
Tying tips: Micro leeches are very simple patterns to tie. Lead weight is not needed because the gold bead makes up for the lead, allowing the pattern to "bob" in the water upon retrieval. To attach a bead, first crimp the hook barb, place the hook in your vise with its eye pointing upward, and then slide the bead (small hole first) over the point, detach the hook and slip the bead up to the eye. Attach your thread behind the bead, and fill in the large-hole cavity with tying thread until the bead doesn't slide.

Alternative colours for micro leeches that work well for me are exactly the same as I use for my Blood Bugger patterns. You can also use other colours of beads (copper, silver, or gun metal) combined with copper, gold and silver ribbing.

Leech, the Bulldog Bead Head

Originator: Brent Schlenker, for his good friend and mine, Dale Freschi (modified & tied by Brian Smith)
Hook: Mustad 9672 #4–10
Head: gold bead
Tail: marabou; body length, colour Superfly Burnt Orange
Hackle: olive-dyed grizzly, palmered over body 6–7 turns
Body: chenille, colour Dragonfly CTM250 Metallic Gold
Comment: A very fast and simple tie, this pattern is named after the "Bulldog" himself, Dale Freschi, my friend and fishing partner in Prince George. Brent Schlenker, amongst other occupations a professional fly tier from Medicine Hat, Alberta, tied the Bulldog to represent small bait fish that big rainbows love to feed on: sculpins, shiners, and perch. If you ever have the pleasure of fishing with Dale, please don't frustrate yourself by trying to keep up with him because you'll soon realize how he received that nickname. He is tenacious in

his pursuit of any fish, be it trout, salmon, bonefish, tarpon or marlin.

If you tie and fish the Bulldog it could change your whole attitude about pattern selections, because it is that good. Dale begins his day with this pattern 80 percent of the time in trout lakes. I've tried to out-fish him many times with my patterns that should work better given the time of year we are fishing, but rarely can anything beat the Bulldog! I believe it's akin to the Woolly Worm, representing leeches, damsels and dragon nymphs as well as bait fishes.

Tying tip: Marabou tails work best when you tie with the whole feather. Choose one that is long and fine at its tips, not fibrous or fuzzy. Strip the fluffy section off the feather and bind it in just behind the bead, wrapping it along the top of the shank to the beginning of the bend. Finally, take 3 turns of thread under the tail fibres and around the hook shank, which helps to keep them from tangling under the hook when retrieved while fishing the swimming pattern.

Chironomid Patterns

Chironomid Larva, Bloodworm Translucent

Originator: Brian Smith 2004
Hook: Tiemco 200R #10–14
Thread: UTC, red
Tail: none
Body: floss red, single strand, 6–7 turns
Ribs: copper wire, fine, tied in front of red floss strand
Underbody: dental floss, wrapped down then up the hook
Topcoat: floss, underbody, and ribs with 2 coats clear nail polish
Hackle: pheasant rump, reddish phase, 1 turn only, hook length

Tying tips: In order to keep the body slim, the first procedure is to tie the rib, red floss and the dental floss behind the hook eye. With the dental floss on top, wrap all materials together to the rear of the shank, and then return the dental floss to the tie-in point. The red floss is wrapped over the dental floss in 6–7 turns, and the ribbing wrapped in front of each turn of floss. I find it easiest to tie and clear coat all the flies that I am tying first, let them set overnight, and then apply the hackle and finish the patterns next day.

Chironomid, Chromie

Originator: Brian Smith 1996
Hook: Tiemco 2457 #12–14
Thread: UTC, black
Underbody: Mylar silver, fine
Ribs: nylon, charcoal, 6–7 turns, followed by red wire; underbody, ribs and wing case top-coated with 1 coat of 5-minute epoxy

Wing case: turkey primary strip, dark
Gills: Antron white, a short tuft each side of hook shank
Thorax: peacock herls; 2, under the wing case
Tying tip: Use the same sequence as the translucent bloodworm, wrapping the hook shank with Mylar, and then bringing the ribs up the shank in progression over the Mylar. The purpose of the Mylar is to imitate the air gas encased in the exoskeleton, serving to create a translucent glossy appearance to the body of the emerging chironomid pupa. When I tie the pupa, I purposely leave only the back half of the insect showing chrome.

Chironomid, CDC Black & Pearl

Originator: Jeff Morgan, USA (modified & tied by Brian Smith 2012)
Hook: Tiemco 2457 #10–16
Thread: UTC, black
Ribs: UTC thread, black; copper wire, x-small; wound over underbody
Underbody: Crystal Flash, pearl
Wing: CDC feather, natural; tied over body at thorax, kept short
Gills: Antron, white; posted behind eye
Thorax: peacock herls
Tying tips: At the ⅔-point of the shank, tie in both ribs and then the Crystal Flash; follow the ribs down and past the hook bend, wrapping them with the Crystal Flash, and then wrap the Crystal Flash back to the tie-in point. Follow with the ribs, the gills and finally the thorax.
Comment: I picked this pattern from the website "Westfly." Jeff Morgan is a regular contributor to the site; he had the thought bubble for the CDC feather. CDC (Cul de Canard), taken from a duck's back, is oily and floats like a cork. Jeff reasons that the CDC will trap air bubbles, replicating the gases that chironomid pupae expel that slowly floats them to the surface as they begin their emergence period. Bravo, Jeff! I'll buy it.

Tie them in several alternative colours of Crystal Hair underbody, keeping the same theme: olive, chartreuse, silver, gold and red. You can also tie them using bead heads, colours silver, copper and gold, which will assist in sinking the pattern quickly, adding that "bobbing" motion when slowly retrieved that fish seem to enjoy striking at, and the pattern will continue as designed to trap air bubbles in the CDC feather.

Chironomid, Emerging Adult

Originator: Brian Smith
Hook: Mustad 94840 #14–16
Tail (as shuck): mallard feather barbules, natural grey
Tag (as gills): ostrich plume barbule, 3 turns
Body: goose primary barbs, grey
Thorax: peacock herl, 2–3 turns
Wing: deer hairs, cinnamon; posted over hook eye, trimmed over thorax
Comment: Have you ever noticed that when chironomids emerge, they look to be a reddish colour? With the cinnamon wing, I have captured the look of the real wing, which turns to grey after drying and before the chironomid leaves the lake's surface.

May
Callibaetis Mayfly Patterns

Mayfly Nymph, Callibaetis Olive

Originator: Brian Smith 1991
Hook: Tiemco 2312 #12–16
Thread: UTC, grey-olive
Tails: grizzly hackle dyed olive; abdomen length
Rib: gold wire, fine, counter-wrapped over abdomen 5–6 turns
Abdomen: goose primary barbs, dyed grey-olive
Wing-case: peacock herls, laid over thorax and hackle
Thorax: rabbit dubbing, dark olive
Hackle: grouse feather dyed olive; tied over thorax "spent style"

Also shown in parachute style.

Tying tips: My favourite size hook for this pattern is #14. The only trick to learn is the laying of a feather hackle over the thorax. Begin by choosing a small whole grouse feather with fibres slightly shorter than the abdomen. Trim the fuzz and excess barbs, leaving about 5 mm of barbs each side of the stem. Spread the barbs backward toward the base of the stem and then tie the remaining tip in front of the wing-case material, glossy side up, before the thorax dubbing is applied. Apply the thorax, and then lay the hackle over the thorax; finally, pull the wing-case material over the thorax and hackle and finish the fly.

If you wish to tie some cinnamon-coloured mayfly nymphs for brackish waters, use the same methods, substituting the following materials: UTC thread, brown; grizzly hackle, brown, for tails; pheasant sword for abdomens; natural brown grouse feathers for hackles and thorax dubbings of SLDW01 Whitlock's Red Fox Squirrel.

Mayfly Adult Dun, Callibaetis Olive

Originator: Brian Smith 2009
Hook: Tiemco 2312 #12–16
Thread: UTC, olive
Tails: moose hairs 4–5; body lengths, spread

Rib: Kevlar thread, white; 4–5 turns over abdomen
Wing: mallard flank feather dyed olive; folded and posted at ⅔-shank point, top clipped to round shape
Abdomen: nylon, olive; tapered larger to front
Thorax: dubbing, Chan's Soft Blend olive; behind and in front of wing
Hackles: grizzly and brown, 1 each; 3–4 turns each, 1 behind wing, 2–3 in front
Tying tips: Posting a mallard wing feather for dry flies takes a little practice, but can be mastered most successfully by choosing the correct feather. Some mallard feathers will be large and have long barbs, ideal for minnow imitations on size #8 hooks; others will be small breast feathers, perfect for size #18–20 hooks. For dry-fly models size #14, choose a whole feather that is medium size, flat on the top and high-quality with not a lot of fuzz. Trim the fuzz from the stem, leaving enough barbules to measure more than body length on the hook.

After the tails are tied in, pinch the feather in the middle with thumb and forefinger to cup the barbules together, measure it on top of the hook to body length, and then bring it forward, tips pointing to the eye to tie the feather at ⅔-shank point of the hook. The key is to never let go of the feather until it is cinched in place. Post it upward by forming a block with tying thread in front and behind the feather, finishing the exercise with several turns around the base of the feather on top of the hook shank.

When installing 2 hackles on a dry fly (which I like to do on most of my dries size #12 and larger) choose saddle or cape hackles by using a hackle gauge or by measuring them to be 1½ times the gap of the hook. One at a time, bind both just in front of the wing, concave (flat) side toward the eye of the hook. Take your first turn of the front hackle north of the shank and behind the wing and then bring it forward 3–4 turns leaving a small gap between turns and finish at least 2 mm behind the eye. Your second hackle will be applied in the same manner, winding it through the first, placing it between the gaps of the first hackle. This method will force your hackles to stand upward supporting each other, preventing them from twisting. Finish the head.

For dry flies that you plan to fish with, turn the hook upside down and trim the hackles under the shank to a V-notch the width of the hook gap, which assists your fly to land and ride upright on the water.

Mayfly Adult Spinner, Callibaetis

Originator: Brian Smith 1994 (modified several times)
Hook: Tiemco 2312 #12–16
Thread: UTC, black
Tails: moose hairs, pale colour, 5–7; body lengths and spread
Rib: Kevlar thread, white, 5–6 turns over abdomen
Wing: mallard flank feather, natural grey; folded and posted upright, clipped to rounded shape
Abdomen: nylon fine, charcoal
Thorax: dubbing, Hare-Tron HT 7 black
Hackles: grizzly saddle (2); 1 wrap each behind wing, 2–3 in front

Spring Mayfly Patterns for Creeks and Rivers

Mayfly Nymph, Flashback Bead Head

Originator: unknown (modified & tied by Brian Smith)
Hook: Tiemco 2457 #12–18
Thread: UTC, brown-olive
Bead head: gold bead, small
Tail: pheasant sword barbs, tied to sweep downward
Rib: gold wire, fine; 5–6 counter-clockwise turns over abdomen
Abdomen: pheasant sword barbs (2), wrapped to wing case
Wing case: pearl Mylar strand
Thorax: peacock herl
Tying tip: To insert a bead, first crimp the hook barb, and then slide the bead to the head, small opening toward the eye. Attach tying thread, fill the cavity of the bead behind it with thread and begin tying your pattern. Finish your pattern and tie off behind the bead.

Mayfly Nymph, Hare's Ear Bead Head

Originator: unknown (modified & tied by Brian Smith)
Comment: Pattern is tied exactly the same as the Flashback Nymph above, but substitute a tail of grouse hackle barbs and abdomen of grey Canada goose primary barbs.

Soft Hackle Emerger

Originator: unknown (modified & tied by Brian Smith)
Hook: Tiemco 2487 #12–18
Thread: UTC, grey-brown
Abdomen: floss, yellow-gold
Thorax: dubbing, natural rabbit under-fur
Hackle: grouse, natural, 1 turn only
Tying tips: I use Tiemco 2487 hooks for my emerger patterns because they are fine wire hooks that will ride currents in the upper water column, as opposed to Tiemco 2457 sinking heavy-wire hooks for my small nymph patterns, which I want to drift near the bottom—a small detail, but often a difference-maker for catching trout.

This soft hackle pattern can be tied in many variations of abdomen colours that imitate emerging mayflies: black, tan, olive, bright yellow, orange and lime green. The trick is to imitate the mayfly or caddis colour that is hatching. This is where familiarity with your rivers comes in—observe or question other fly fishers about colours that catch trout and duplicate them often.

Soft hackle patterns also replicate caddis emergers—use them in any non-hatch activities or during a hatch when trout are fussy and refuse to rise.

Mayfly Adult Dun, Blue-Winged Olive (BWO) Quill

Originator: Brian Smith 2011
Hook: Tiemco 2312 #16–18
Thread: UTC, brown-olive
Tails: moose hairs, pale; body lengths, spread
Underbody: UTC thread, brown-olive
Rib: marabou quill stripped, light olive, wrapped 5–6 turns over abdomen underbody
Wing: mallard flank feather dyed grey; body length, posted at ⅔-point of shank
Abdomen: underbody of UTC brown-olive threads
Thorax: dubbing, Whitlock's SLF SLDW06 olive
Hackles (2): grizzly saddle; 1 turn each behind wing, 2–3 turns in front
Comment: This pattern can be tied traditionally (as listed above) or in parachute style, and is a nice improvement over one that I developed ten years ago. This is a terrific fly pattern for early spring and late fall fly fishing.

My Adams

Originator: Brian Smith 2011 (revision of 1992 pattern)
Hook: Tiemco 2312 #16–22
Thread: UTC, grey-brown
Tail: grizzly and brown hackles, mixed
Wing: mallard flank feather, natural; body length, folded and posted at ⅔-shank point
Abdomen: primary goose barb, natural grey
Thorax: dubbing, Hare-Tron Hare's Ear Plus colour HET 2 Dark Hare's Ear
Hackles (2): grizzly and brown; 1 turn each behind wing, 3–4 turns in front
Comment: This is a midge pattern you cannot be without in your fly box, because it represents everything tiny that hatches from both lakes and rivers. I like them in traditional style for sizes 14–16, and parachute style for 18–20 using Mustad 94840 hooks and Orvis 4641 "Big Eye" for size 22.

Adams, Quill Dun

Originator: Brian Smith 2012
Hooks: Tiemco 2312 #16–18; Mustad 94840 #20–22
Thread: UTC, grey-brown
Tails: moose hairs, body lengths
Wing: mallard feather, natural; posted at ⅔-shank point
Body: marabou quill, dyed grey; tied over underbody of UTC thread, grey-brown
Thorax: dubbing, Hare-Tron Hare's Ear Plus colour HET 2 Dark Hare's Ear
Hackles (2): grizzly and brown; 1 turn each behind wing, 2 turns in front
Comment: I've carried this pattern forward and adapted it from the series of mayfly quill bodies that A.K. Best is famous for. I really like it on the Adams, and will also show it tied parachute style, especially for hook sizes #20–22. It's a reliable substitute for adult midges and BWOs.

June
Caddis Patterns for Still Waters

Caddis Larva, Woolly Worm

Originator: unknown (tied by Brian Smith)
Hook: Mustad 9672 #8–10
Thread: UTC, olive
Tail: hackle barbs, brown
Hackle: brown, hook gap length; palmered over body, trimmed to hook gap
Body: chenille, olive or tan-brown
Comment: The Woolly Worm has been around and in fly tiers' boxes for at least fifty years. It's a fine imitation for anything that looks like larvae—caterpillars, caddis larvae, rock worms, scuds if small enough, and even leeches if the hackle is long and flowing—fish seem to relish the looks they impart. They are the first fly patterns an instructor teaches a budding fly tier because they are simple to tie and catch fish regardless of how poor they look when they come from the vise.

Caddis Pupa, Traveler Sedge

Originator: Jack Shaw circa 1970s (modified & tied by Brian Smith)
Hook: Tiemco 200R or 2312 #8–12
Thread: UTC, light olive
Rib: rod-building thread, yellow-gold
Underbody: lead wire, .020 mm, wrapped on rear half of hook, followed by embroidery threads, olive; build fatter at the rear, tapered to front, coat with

head cement and flatten appearance by squeezing with pliers

Abdomen: dubbing, Hare-Tron HT 19 Dark Olive

Wing case: deer hairs dyed cinnamon, tied over thorax

Eyes: Larva Lace or V-rib: lashed behind hook eye; burn ends to thorax width

Thorax: dubbing, colour SLF 37 Rust Brown

Swimmerets: golden pheasant tippet barbs; 4–6 on each side of shank in front of thorax, protruding outward and swept back to almost abdomen length

Antennae: pheasant rump, green phase; body length, a few barbs each side of thorax, swept back

Head: dubbing, SLF 37 Rust Brown, lashed around eyes

Comment: This is a time-consuming fly to tie, but will hold up for many trout, as the rougher and more beat-up it gets, the better it seems to work. It's a fun pattern to tie because of its colour varieties and general attraction to the angler—one of my favourites.

Also shown: egg-laying Mikulak with green egg-sac butt.

Caddis Adult, Mikulak Traveler Sedge

Originator: Art Mikulak, Calgary AB (modified & tied by Brian Smith)

Hook: Tiemco 2312 #8–14

Thread: Uni-mono, clear

Tail: deer hairs, natural: 8–10 hairs, stacked; tied to extend ⅓-body length

Body: dubbing, Haretron Hare's Ear Plus, colour HET2 Dark Hare's Ear: 2–3 turns between stacks of deer hair

Wings: deer hairs, natural; stacked, 4 sections in front of dubbing for sizes 8 and 10 hooks; 3 sections for size 12–14

Hackles (2): grizzly and brown mixed; 3–4 turns each in front of last wing

Tying tips: This is a pattern that will frustrate the beginning fly tier, but is an essential fly to have in your arsenal for representing the traveller sedge caddis fly on still waters. There are several key tricks I have learned over the years that will help you master the steps of tying this fly with deer hair. When well tied, a Mikulak will hold up for ten to twenty fish; exchange it every half-dozen fish or so to let the first fly dry.

Thread: use clear mono, which can be tightened firmer than nylon threads. Quantity: use only about a 4-mm width of deer hair for each wing and tail section. Quality: use only long, select deer hairs for Mikulaks. Tail: deer hairs must be tied tightly to the hook shank, otherwise they will spin. Stacking: use a deer hair stacker and a nit comb to remove underhairs. Tightness: use a soft loop for your first turn on a section of deer hairs for wings, gradually apply more pressure, and make the last turns very tight.

Begin this pattern with your thread at the ¾-point of the shank; bind the tail hairs at this spot and wrap over them tightly all the way down the shank. Wrap up and down the shank, binding tightly until you cannot spin the hairs on the shank. Take a few final turns under the tail hairs to set them upward. Next, two to three turns of dubbing, then a 4-mm section of deer hair that ends exactly at the end of the tail hairs; trim and repeat sequence 3–4 times (3 stacks for hook sizes #12–14; 4 stacks for sizes #8–10) with dubbing and deer hairs, ending at the ¾-point of the shank. Bind 2 hackles in front of the last wing section (grizzly first, brown last), concave (flat) side facing the hook eye; take 3–4 turns each grizzly and brown hackles. Finish your fly.

Lastly, turn the fly upside down and clip a V-notch the width of the hook gap out of the hackles, which will allow the imitation caddis to ride upright on its outside hackles. Failure to do this exercise will result in your fly flopping to its side or riding on an angle.

Caddis, Goddard's

Originator: John Goddard (tied by Brian Smith)
Hook: Tiemco 2312 #10–14
Thread: Uni-mono, clear
Body: deer hairs; 5–6 sections tied and allowed to spin on hook, trimmed to caddis tent-like shape, fatter at the rear of the fly
Antennae (2): brown hackle stems, more than body lengths; stripped, tied and curled in front of hook eye
Hackle: brown saddle, 5–6 turns
Tying tips: This one takes a little practice, especially the trimming of spun deer hair. I like to spin a bunch of bodies, tie them off, put them aside, and then trim all of them in the same session and finish the flies.

Begin with a pencil-width section of deer hair, lash it figure-eight on top of the hook shank at the bend of your hook, tighten very securely and let the hairs spin around the shank. Repeat the process 5–6 times, compressing each section tightly against the last with your thumb or a compression tool.

To trim the body to shape, use a combination of curved scissors and a single-edge razor blade. First, trim the underside flat to the shank. Next, carefully shape the body in a triangular fashion, wide base at the bottom, leaving trailing hairs out the rear of the fly. For the final trim, I find that taking the fly out of the vise and turning the hook eye away from me when trimming helps to conquer the procedure.

The antennae are curled by pulling them tightly with your thumbnail and first finger, and then trim them to equal lengths.

Comment: This fly pattern has been around for at least forty years. John Goddard is credited with its design and creation. It floats like a cork and has been a productive caddis searching pattern for a long time. I like sizes #8 and 10 for lakes, dropping to sizes #12 and 14 for river fishing.

Damselfly

Damselfly Nymph

Originator: Jack Shaw circa 1960s (modified & tied by Brian Smith 1992; modified many times since)
Hook: Tiemco 200R #10–12
Thread: UTC, watery olive
Tails: grizzly hackle barbs dyed olive; good bunch, ½-body length, splayed
Ribs: rod-building thread, yellow-gold; 6–7 ribs over abdomen
Abdomen: dubbing, Chan's Soft Blend, olive
Wing case: deer hairs dyed olive; wrapped over thorax and tied off behind eyes
Hackle: grizzly hackle feather dyed olive; palmered through thorax, bottom and top of barbules clipped, barbs remaining extended perpendicular to body
Eyes: Larva Lace, olive, body width; burn ends
Thorax: dubbing, Chan's Soft Blend, olive; also wrap figure-eight over and around eyes after the wing case is tied down

Tying tips: This pattern has a lot of steps, but if you tie it in the sequence listed you should have fun and no trouble with it. I list my version of this pattern as originating in 1992. I have adapted my pattern to use Brian Chan's Soft Blend dubbing, which hasn't been around for twenty years, but it's the best-looking (and performing) new material I've come across.

If you tie its eyes after the thorax and hackle, you'll likely fry your hackle and thorax when you burn its eyes. . . just a tip, I've done it. I like to clip the palmered hackle barbs after tying the fly. The natural swims with its legs outward, perpendicular to its body, and paddles frantically—I'd be in a hurry too!

The colour of the nymph can be altered to represent the olive-brown colouration often found in brackish water. Substitute Whitlock's SLF colour SLDW12 Damsel Tan with brown hackles for tails and legs and you've got it.

My concept of using deer hairs for the wing case deserves mention. Being hollow and buoyant, it aids to float my pattern over weed-infested shoals and marl bottoms, and through reeds and stalks, allowing extra precious time for imitating the swimming nymph with floating or intermediate sink lines.

Dragonfly Nymph, Darner

Originator: Jack Shaw circa 1970s (version modified & tied by Brian Smith 2009)
Hook: Tiemco 200R #6–12
Thread: UTC, olive
Tails: moose hairs, dark; tied short as stub, splayed
Ribs: gold wire, medium; 5–6 turns over abdomen
Underbody: .020 lead wires, wrapped over rear ½ of hook shank, over-wrapped with olive embroidery threads; coat with head cement and flatten appearance with pliers
Abdomen: seal fur dubbing, dark olive
Wing case: moose hairs; over thorax and eyes, then back again and clipped (last tying procedure)
Eyes: V-rib, grey-olive; burned body width, wrapped with peacock herl after thorax and second set of legs are tied
Legs: moose hairs, in front of wing case on each side; sweep back to abdomen length
Thorax: seal fur dubbing dark olive
More legs: moose hairs, in front of thorax; tied under body, swept back body length
Comment: I weight the body to get the nymph to the bottom zone, but utilize moose hairs in the pattern to float it off the bottom muck and weed cover much like Alf Davey explained when he developed the Bottom Walker in the 1970s.

Another colour I use is Ligas 42 olive-grey, which simulates the moulting nymph's period when its soft exoskeleton is exposed and often becomes preferred table fare for trout.

Tying tips: see Damsel Nymph pattern; the difficult steps are similar.

Dragonfly Nymph, Red-Shouldered

Originator: Jack Shaw circa 1960s (version modified &
tied by Brian Smith 2009)
Hook: Mustad 94840 #6–8
Thread: UTC, olive
Tails: moose hairs, pale; tied short as stub, splayed
Ribs: gold wire, medium, 5–6 turns over abdomen
Underbody: .020 lead wires wrapped rear ½ of shank;
over-wrapped with olive embroidery thread; coat with head cement and flatten
appearance with pliers
Abdomen: dubbing, colour Dragonfly SCD259 Light Scud
Wing case: moose hairs; over thorax
Eyes: V-rib grey-olive; burned body width, wrapped with dubbing Dragonfly
SCD259 after thorax and second set of legs are tied (last tying procedure)
Legs: moose hairs, in front of wing case on each side; sweep back to abdomen length
Thorax: dubbing, Dragonfly SCD259
More legs: moose hairs; in front of thorax, tied under body, swept back body length
Comment: Red-shouldered dragonfly nymphs are much lighter in colour than
darners, most often a grey-olive, and quite stubby and hairy in appearance. In
my first book, *Fly Fishing BC's Interior*, I showed you the all-deer-hair version
of the red-shouldered nymph, which I mistakenly called the Gomphus (as Jack
Shaw did), and was corrected by several experts in the field of entomology. This
is an alternative model, using dubbing, and I use them both. The tying steps for
darners and red-shouldered are similar; if you can follow the steps for the darner,
the red-shouldered nymph is a simple spinoff.

July
Caddis Fly

Caddis Adult Spotted, DH Emerger

Originator: Brent Schlenker, Medicine Hat, AB (modi-
fied & tied by Brian Smith 2005)
Hook: Mustad 94840 #16–18
Thread: UTC, grey-brown
Trailing shuck: Antron, rust, body length
Hackle: brown saddle, palmered through body dry

style; trimmed to hook gap

Body: dubbing, Haretron Hare's Ear Plus, colour HET 2 Dark Hare's Ear

Wing: deer hairs, natural: stack, over body only; clump left over eye of hook, trimmed at 45° angle

Tying tips: When tying deer hair patterns smaller than size 14, I like to use medium-length leg hairs from the deer's skin, which are shorter and finer than those found on the deer's back, rump or shoulder (which I use for Mikulak Travelers). Elk hair is also good, stiffer than deer, more hollow and floats well, but it's difficult to find in short, fine skins.

Comment: Al Troth, USA, was the designer of the original Elk Hair Caddis fly pattern. When you design fly patterns, all it takes sometimes is a colour variation and small deviation from a standard pattern, such as adding a trailing shuck, to entice and trigger a response from your quarry. This is not to suggest there is anything wrong with an original pattern, because who knows what a trout is thinking at the time? A fly fisher meets many circumstances on the water when standard imitations don't work, and you have to improvise—such is the birth of new variations.

This pattern has proven deadly for me when finicky trout are taking an emerging hatch of caddis. The trailing shuck must suggest a "cripple" to trout, or a caddis struggling to be free of its shuck, an insect that is plowing water and creating disturbance from both ends of its body. Dale Freschi uses variations of this pattern given him by Brent extensively in the Bow and Crowsnest rivers.

I tie these small caddis flies in several other colour combinations of shuck and dubbing: Antron colour "rust" shuck, cinnamon body; olive shuck, caddis green body; rust shuck, dark brown-olive body (Grannom). You can also substitute bleached deer hairs for natural to imitate common species of pale-winged caddis, and come up with a fabulous-looking little fish catcher that I call a "Blondie."

I was into a hatch of pale caddis on the Bow River late one afternoon several years ago, and took plump rainbows on nine successive casts with this blonde pattern when nothing else would work. The "Blondie" is also a great pattern for low-light conditions, as it is highly visible amidst foam and other insects hatching during late-summer evenings.

Caddis Adult, "Blondie" Emerger

Originator: Brent Schlenker, Medicine Hat, AB (modified & tied by Brian Smith 2005)
Thread: UTC, tan
Hook: Mustad 94840 #16–18
Trailing shuck: Antron, rust colour, body length
Hackle: brown, palmered through body
Body: dubbing, Dragonfly SCD 041 Tan
Wing: deer hairs bleached: stacked, over body only; clump left over eye of hook, trimmed at 45° angle

Stoneflies

Stonefly Adult, Salmon Fly

Originator: Pat Barnes Sofa Pillow pattern circa 1940s (modified & tied by Brian Smith 1995)
Hook: Tiemco 2312 #4–8
Thread: UTC, orange
Tail: elk hairs, natural dark; short tail, slightly past hook bend
Ribs: rod building thread, yellow-gold; 5–6 turns, followed by a turn of peacock herl in front of each thread wrap
Abdomen: floss, orange
Wing: elk hairs, natural dark; extended over body to end of tail
Antennae: marabou quills (2), black, stripped; body lengths, one each side of hook eye
Thorax: dubbing, Hare-Tron HE 17 Rusty Orange
Hackles: brown (2); 5–6 turns through thorax dubbing
Tying tips: It's hard for beginning tiers to keep a fly body slim when you put four separate items at the bend of the hook shank. To accomplish a trim, neat look on my flies, I begin by starting the tail hairs at the ⅔-point of the hook shank, tie them on top of the hook, wrap all the way to the bend and then make 2 wraps under the tail hairs at the bend to posture the tail in an upward direction. Now wrap the hairs very tightly back to the tie-in point

and return to the bend; if your wraps are not tight enough, the tail will spin during the rest of the operation.

Tie the ribs in at the bend and wrap your thread back to the ⅔-starting point. Secure the floss, wrap to the bend and return with the floss to the starting point. Your ribs follow next, and your fly's body has no lumps. Use this method for all of your ribbed patterns and you'll keep a slim profile on your flies.

Comment: When I designed this pattern in 1995, I fashioned it after the famed "Improved" Sofa Pillow (originally designed by Pat Barnes in the 1940s), which is a successful standby model in Montana and Idaho rivers. Stonefly adults have muted tones on their bellies with bright markings on heads and thoraxes. I felt I needed to add some colour and flair to the standard pattern, so I played with dark and light ribbings to create a colour scheme that suggests subtle hints of contrast. I think my forty-five years of working in the paint and coatings business has left me dabbling with ideas that surprise me sometimes.

Patterns for Golden Stones and Skwalas are takeoffs from this one. For the Golden Stone, substitute yellow-gold floss and thorax dubbing Hare-Tron HT-10 Golden Stone; for Skwala, brown-olive floss and thorax Hare-Tron HT-10.

Mayfly

Mayfly Adult Dun, Western Green Drake Quill

Originator: A.K. Best, USA (modified & tied by Brian Smith 2009)
Hook: Tiemco 2312 #12–16
Thread: UTC, grey-brown
Tails: moose hairs: body lengths, splayed
Abdomen underbody: UTC tying threads, grey-brown
Rib: marabou quill: light olive, wrapped over underbody
Wing: mallard flank feather dyed Western Green Drake, posted
Hackles (2): grizzly and brown; 5 turns each over thorax, 2 behind wing, 3 in front
Thorax: dubbing, rabbit: dark olive
Tying tips: To post a mallard feather, refer again to p. 92, where I discussed the method of choosing and posting a mallard feather for the Mayfly Adult, Callibaetis.
Comment: This pattern can be tied in traditional or

parachute styles with the same dressings. For parachute styles I use only one hackle, either grizzly or brown, which keeps the pattern sparse.

The Flavilinea drake can be represented by this same model, but tie it in sizes #14 and 16 and substitute mallard feather, colour dun, for the wing. Mayfly patterns have been around for hundreds of years, the use of quills perhaps fifty to seventy years. I'm giving the great US fly tier and designer A.K. Best some credit for this pattern, if only because his variety of quill patterns was the first and best I came across. Naturally, I had to fool around with A.K.'s patterns because that's in my fly-fishing genetic makeup (changing things, being creative); it was, however, his thought bubble I took it from.

Mayfly Adult Dun, Brown Drake Quill

Top row, from left: two variations of the Brown Drake Quill; Pale Morning Dun Quill. Bottom, from left: Pale Morning Dun Quill Parachute; Trico Parachute.

Originator: A.K. Best, USA (modified & tied by Brian Smith 2009)
Hook: Tiemco 2312 #10–12
Thread: UTC, brown
Tails: moose hairs: body lengths, splayed
Abdomen underbody: UTC tying threads, brown
Ribs: marabou quills (2): rust brown and yellow-olive, wrapped over underbody
Wing: mallard flank feather dyed dun, posted
Hackles (2): grizzly and brown; 5 turns each over thorax: 2 behind wing, 3 in front
Thorax: dubbing, colour Hare-Tron HT16 Dark Brown

August

Salmon Bucktail for Salt Water

Originator: unknown (modified & tied by Brian Smith 2010)
Hooks (2): Gamakatsu Octopus 02013 #1/0–3/0; stinger hook attached with Tuf-Line 12-kg test
Body: Mylar braid, silver; parted, lengths of both hooks
Wings and flash (in order): polar bear, red bucktail, Polar Flash and Icelandic Sheep, olive; laid over body, full lengths of both hooks

Head: black
Eyes: prismatic eyes, silver; 1 each side, head and eyes coated with 5-minute epoxy
Tying tips: The first tip is how to attach a stinger hook to your front hook. I use Tuf-Line wire leader material, about a 10-cm length. Double the wire and with strong fly-tying monocord, lash it securely, beginning slightly behind the hook eye, to the bend of the hook and back again. Tie off, and coat the wrapping lash with 5-minute epoxy, set aside until dry. Your stinger hook is attached by inserting the wire tag end into the eye of your second hook and then looping and securing the trailing hook into the wire.

The Mylar for the body is hollow, and is threaded over the body from the eye, cut and attached at the eye and then parted with a dubbing needle so the rear strands from the front hook separate and flare the lengths of both hooks.

The hair winging material is attached behind the hook eye one at a time, and trimmed at the head on a 45° angle to keep the head buildup from becoming too bulky.

Comment: Bucktail flies are easy and fun to tie. If you do a fair amount of salmon fishing, and when you consider the cost of buying them at a ten-spot each, it doesn't take much in the way of fly-tying materials to recoup your money layout.

If you can find long, glossy polar bear hair, buy it, because it's probably the most sought-after material for all patterns of salmon and steelhead flies that use white in their patterns. Its iridescence and light reflectivity in the water is amazing, and cannot be duplicated by any other natural hair.

You can tie bucktail patterns in a variety of colours, all using polar bear and Polar or Krystal Flash as base colours, complementing them with bucktail colours of blue, chartreuse, pink, yellow and red, or combinations of these colours depending on which baitfish you are trying to replicate.

Caddis Fly

Caddis Adult, Grannom DH Emerger

Originator: Brent Schlenker, Medicine Hat, AB (modified & tied by Brian Smith 2010)
Hook: Mustad 94840 #16–18
Thread: UTC, grey-brown
Trailing shuck: Antron, rust colour, body length
Hackle: brown saddle, palmered through body dry style; trimmed to hook gap
Body: dubbing, Hare-Tron HT 16 Dark Brown
Wing: deer hairs, natural dark: stack, over body; clump left over eye of hook, trimmed at 45° angle
Tying tips: See p. 102 for tying tips on this emerger pattern.

Caddis Adult, October Mikulak

Originator: Art Mikulak, Calgary, AB (modified & tied by Brian Smith)
Hook: Tiemco 2312 #10–14
Thread: Uni-mono, clear
Tail: deer hairs, cinnamon; stacked, tied short (about ⅓-body length)
Body: dubbing, Whitlock's SLF 37 Rust Brown; 4 clumps for size 10, 3 for sizes 12 and 14, alternated between deer-hair wings
Wing(s): deer hairs, cinnamon; 3–4 stacks depending on hook size
Hackles (2): brown, 3–4 turns each
Tying tips: for complete tying instructions, see Caddis Adult, Mikulak Sedge, p. 97.

Hoppers

Foam Hopper

Originator: Brian Smith 2012 (adapted from my earlier versions)
Hook: Tiemco 2312 #6–12
Thread: Uni-mono, clear
Tail: none
Rib: none
Underbody and protrusion: foam strip, layered brown over tan; extended body length beyond hook shank
Body: dubbing, Hare-Tron HET 2 Dark Hare's Ear Plus; over underbody (body section only)
Wings: turkey primary sections, oak colour; one each side of body, extended half over underbody protrusion
Wings supplement: moose hairs; bunch laid over wings
Legs (2): brown hackle feathers, clipped and knotted; swept back to end of hook shank, tips pointed downward
Head: deer hairs, natural; spun and clipped bullet shape
Tying tips: This pattern is not as difficult as it looks, although time-consuming with its many components. I purchase sheets of foam at Walmart's notion department, cut them in 3-mm strips with a sharp blade, and then Krazy Glue them together, brown over tan, or brown over yellow. Be careful when gluing not to touch glue skin to skin! Have some acetone handy to clean your fingers.

Use Mono-thread, and begin the underbody at the ⅔-point of the shank; wrap it tightly backward and forward several times—when secure, it will not spin on the shank. For wings, cut turkey from the quill feather in 5-mm strips; attach one each side of the body, layering them flat by using a soft loop first turn of thread, and then increasing tension toward the hook eye.

Legs are a clipped whole hackle feather—this is a good place to use cape and saddle feathers that are oversized and useless for dry hackles. Spread the hackle barbs toward the stem and clip them about 3 mm wide. Perform an overhand knot at about the halfway point of the clipped feather and pull it tight, which should point the tip to a downward angle. Attach using a soft loop, and then tighten progressively, pointing the leg tips downward.

For the bullet head, use a 5-mm section of deer hairs. Lay it over the shank in front of the wings, figure-eight loosely and let it spin, and then tighten by wrapping thread through the spun clump. Compress the clumps rearward with thumb pressure. The head takes about 3–4 sections to complete. To trim, use heavy curved scissors. First, clip flat the bottom of the deer hairs on the hook shank, then trim the top and sides on an upward angle from the hook eye backward. Lastly, remove the hook from the vise and clean up the head by clipping the deer hairs back to front of the hook eye. It takes a few practice runs to get good at this.

September
Water Boatman and Backswimmer

Water Boatman

Originator: Brian Smith 2011 (modified from earlier patterns)
Hook: Mustad 94840 #12–14
Thread: UTC, tan

Wing case: pheasant sword strip, dark reddish-brown; over body and eyes; coat with clear 5-minute epoxy after fly is finished
Eyes: V-rib, dark reddish brown; burn ends
Body: embroidery threads, pale yellow; over-wrapped with clear Midge-flex, squeeze to flat appearance with pliers
Swimmerets: peacock herl strand, inserted mid-point of body; fixed in place with Krazy Glue, trimmed past body length
Tying tips: The trick for tying this fly is about proportions. Try not to crowd the head, leaving room for finishing the fly with epoxy which, once dry, you'll have a hard time penetrating if you coat the hook eye with cement.

First, tie in the wing case material and clear Midge-flex, wrapping them halfway down the bend of the shank to create a full back. Next, attach the eye material with figure-eight wraps and burn the ends to a fat, blunt appearance. The body is built to a "fat look" with two strands of embroidery thread, built thicker in the middle; it's over-wrapped with the Midge-flex and then squeezed with pliers to flatten and widen the bug's appearance.

To attach the swimmerets, use a stiff piece of peacock herl about 3–4 cm long. Insert the herl into the head of a large sewing needle. Using your pliers, poke the needle through the body above the hook shank slightly in front of mid-point and detach the herl from the needle leaving the herl in the body. Pull the herl from the body a few centimetres, coat it at mid-point with Krazy Glue, reinsert it back into the body and then squeeze with pliers to secure the legs. Trim them 3 mm beyond the body.

I like to finish a half-dozen flies before coating with 5-minute epoxy, as the epoxy dries quickly, and you'll only have time to finish a few flies before it begins to set. I use a dubbing needle to apply the glue, and have lacquer thinner and a rag on hand to clean as I go.

Ants

Ant, Foam Back Black/Orange

Originator: Brian Smith 2010 (adapted from earlier versions)
Hook: Mustad 94840 #14–18
Thread: UTC, black
Abdomen: foam strip, black; tied in, and then covered with dubbing, Hare-Tron HT 7, black
Wing: Antron, grey; in front of and length of abdomen
Thorax: dubbing, Hareline HE17, rusty orange
Hackle: grizzly, palmered through thorax
Tying tips: For foam strips, I purchase a package of multi-coloured inexpensive foam sheets from Walmart or a craft store, and then cut them with a knife to about 2-mm width.

Tie the foam in first, at about the ⅔-point of the hook shank, where the thorax will begin. Bind the foam past the bend of the hook, dub over the abdomen, and tie off. Attach wing material and grizzly saddle hackle, dub the thorax, palmer the hackle and finish the fly.

Alternative colours for ants are all-black and all-orange, the latter using brown saddle instead of grizzly.

Steelhead Flies

Steelhead Intruder

Originator: unknown (modified & tied by Brian Smith 2009)
Hook: Tiemco 9395 or Partridge #01–03
Thread: UTC, black
Tail: rabbit strip, black; extended hook-length past tail
Body: rabbit strip, black; wrapped palmer-style around hook shank
Hackles and flash (in sequence): 4 strands each, body and tail lengths; Flashabou purple on top of shank; holographic blue on bottom
Collar: purple-dyed guinea, 4 turns
Collar: blue-dyed mallard flank, 4 turns
Collar: guinea, natural, 2 turns

Comment: This pattern is mostly seen in fly shops tied with a stinger-style trailing hook and sometimes with barbell eyes. If you're tying these for fishing in BC, you can fish one hook only, so you'll have to cut the front hook flush with the shank. I hate casting flies that have double hooks (the way I dislike using split shot on my tippets), so have designed my pattern to look like them but cast in a more civilized manner. It's your choice to tie this pattern with or without the trailing hook.

I've also designed an alternative smaller version of this fly for use when the water is low and gin-clear on very bright days, and when steelheads are spooked by the intrusion of large flies into their zones. I tie these on #02410 Octopus-style hooks, sizes 1 and 1/0, using the same sequences as above, but substituting Ice Dub UV Black for the dubbed body instead of rabbit strip, which keeps a slimmer appearance.

Egg Fly

Hook: Mustad 9174 #2–4
Thread: UTC, red
Egg: Glo-yarn, bubble-gum pink
Collar: Glo-yarn, white
Tying tips: This is an easy pattern to tie, the only issue

getting the "egg" trimmed correctly. Use a full piece of Glo-yarn about 3 cm long, lash it figure-eight to the top of the hook shank. Next, with your index finger and thumb, grasp the yarn, hold tightly and pull the yarn upward. With curved scissors make one cut underneath your grip on the Glo-yarn; release and the yarn should be a rounded egg shape on top of the hook shank. Turn the hook over in your vise and repeat the procedure on the bottom of the hook shank.

For the collar skein, use a 3-cm piece of white yarn, lash it evenly to the top of the hook behind the eye, spread it around the front of the egg, top and bottom with your fingers and then tie it securely and trim to egg's length.

Comment: This fly can be tied for any egg imitation, varying the colours and hook sizes. For the fall Stellako River sockeye run, I use sockeye red colour and tie these patterns using Tiemco #2457 hooks in sizes #14 and 16.

Mikulak, Rusty Skater

Originator: Art Mikulak, Calgary, AB (modified & tied by Brian Smith)
Hook: Tiemco 2312 #6–8
Thread: Uni-mono, clear
Tail: deer hairs, ½-body length
Tag: dubbing; seal fur, yellow
Body: dubbing, seal fur, rusty red
Wings: deer hairs; 3–4 bunches tied Mikulak style (see tying tips for Caddis Adult, Mikulak Traveler Sedge, p. 97); leave last section of hair untrimmed at hook eye when tying and trim to point upward
Hackles (2): brown saddles, tied dry-style between last section of hair and eye
Comment: This pattern is a great skater, and can be riffle-hitched to improve its waking capacity. To riffle-hitch a fly, the hook eye facing river left, simply throw a half hitch onto the right-hand side of the pattern with your tippet material. The skating action of a riffle-hitched fly across a river seam will often make the difference to a steelhead that wants to be aroused.

Alternative colours and combinations are any that you can dream up. I've had most success with both this colour and olive-dun.

July: The Feast Continues

As I reminisce about the twenty-odd Julys I have spent in the north, it's by far the month with the most favourable conditions for all species of sport fish we have in the North Country: trout, salmon, steelhead and grayling. It's also the most predictable month of the year for weather and the opportunity to fish every type of water: creeks and rivers, saltwater ocean and freshwater lakes. If I were a tourist planning the trip of a lifetime to northern British Columbia or even a resident thinking out a fishing vacation, my best bet would be placed on July.

Why? July is our most temperate month, averaging daytime highs of 22°C and evening lows of just 8°C. It's those single-digit evening lows that keep northerners from growing great tomato crops without a greenhouse. However, it's wonderfully cool for sleeping at night, and the fresh night chills keep our still-water fisheries producing great-tasting trout year-round—you'll rarely come across a "muddy-tasting" fish in the north.

Creeks and rivers are dropping into perfect conditions in July. All of them are open to fishing, so whether you wish to wander up some little roadside stream you have come across, or four-wheel into more difficult terrain to get at the headwaters of rivers you wish to explore, our part of the world is open to you. "Moving" water is running clear in July, warming daily, and will offer some of the most spectacular hatches of the season: stoneflies; summer mayflies, the green and brown drakes; midges; and my personal favourites, caddis flies.

Northwestern BC is blessed with arguably the world's best easily accessible sport saltwater fishery. Inside the great mysterious depths of the Pacific Ocean, the inlets and passages of Chatham Sound, and the rivers of Work, Douglas and Portland channels are gearing up for the great salmon runs of the northwest: springs, sockeyes, cohos, chums and pinks; and migrating with them is the most prized game fish of all for a freshwater angler—the steelhead.

Our coastal northwest is a mecca of great rivers and captivating fishing lore. Most famous and mighty is the Skeena River and some of its legendary tributaries—Kalum, Babine, Kispiox, Copper (Zymoetz), Lakelse, Nass and Bulkley, to name a few, and all of their tributaries. Another important sport fishery is the Kitimat River, which empties into Douglas Channel about 60 km southwest of Terrace.

Another remote river or creek enters the end of each channel and inlet of Chatham Sound; into each the spawning runs continue for great salmon and steelhead, carrying on the procreating rituals of their species. Some years are better than others. With Pacific salmon, when one species is abundant, the other regresses and vice versa. But always in the north, healthy salmon runs mean strong and vigorous lives for every living thing that is nourished by the protein of the salmon's life and death—all species of fish and aquatic life, every class and genera of wildlife.

For still-water lakes, July is a month of climax. All the major spring hatches have culminated. Chironomid activity is on the wane, and won't be a key factor in your fishing successes again until later in the year; mayflies will still hatch sporadically during cool weather spells, often during a rainstorm; and damsel migrations are hit and miss for the angler. Big traveller sedges and dragonfly nymphs will continue to produce well, and trout are still looking for them as they constitute a large meal for foraging fish. Your best bet, however, for trout-fishing lakes is to go back to the staples of the insect orders: leeches, scuds and many of the impressionistic fly patterns such as Spratleys, Careys and more recently, the Bulldog (see p. 87).

Brian Nyberg enjoying some evening solitude on Bridge Lake, Cariboo Region. Glenn Gerbrandt photo.

And you must never forget the Mikulak sedge (see p. 97), my favourite pattern for waking up trout that are looking for a meal on the surface. In high-altitude Cariboo lakes and some of our remote lakes on the north side of Prince George, where summers are short and cool except for a few weeks, July is the best month. Caddis fishing on the surface will invoke memories that will last you a lifetime.

For me, July is the month that I return to rivers and, perhaps except for a few forays with my buddies to the Cariboo and our northernmost lakes, I'll stay there until late September frosts and the nuptial flights of water boatmen drag me off to still waters again, especially to Dragon Lake and its bounty of well-fed trophy rainbows.

Fishing Places

July trout fishing can be spectacular in the North Country, salmon fishing in the Skeena system second to none, and family camping and vacation time in our backcountry some of the very best the world has to offer.

For me, finding the time to crowd everything I wish to do into July and August is an arduous task, akin to tax time, a chore you don't wish to start but look forward to the outcome with eager anticipation and hopeful beginnings through good planning. My Julys are full of outdoor activities, which mostly revolve around fishing, camping, speed boating with my wife, Lois, and finding the opportunity to take a few weeks of vacation time from work to go sailing with our good neighbours, Dwaine and Sandra Harvey, or exploring with family. And July always means my annual excursion to Alberta to fish the Bow River and streams of the southern Alberta foothills, or—in recent years—a foray into the Kootenays to fish the Elk River system with my adult sons, Kevin and Graham.

It seems I never have enough time during July and August to fit the fishing expeditions I wish to take into these two short months. The list of river exploits is endless, many not achievable on an annual basis, but always etched on my mind, many remaining on my bucket list year after year.

By late July, the Crooked is pretty much over most years because of low water conditions, but other northern rivers and their tributaries are in their best conditions, such as Stellako, McLeod, Nation, Parsnip, Middle and Tachie, to name the best of the numerous. The North Cariboo and Chilcotin rivers are also producing at their best—Blackwater, Horsefly, Canim, Quesnel, Chilcotin and Dean—their names synonymous with fabulous fly-fishing water.

I am haunted by rivers, their enchanting mysteries of flow and personalities, endless cycles of change, and forever the challenge of fishing them. They are never constant in their quest for reproduction. You may think for a fleeting morning you have a river figured out, and in the afternoon the trout abruptly alter their cycles, making your morning success but a memory, a time and place in history. The fish, however, are predictable. Once you discover a pattern, colour and size that works on a river, it will always work given the same time of year and circumstances.

Each river has its own individuality and quirks, which are yours to discover as a fly fisher, yours to mould to your own thinking if you wish, because once befriended they reach to your inner self and you are obsessed with their secrets. Uncover and solve them, and you are becoming a complete fly fisher.

Unless we have an extended July hot weather spell that lasts several weeks, lakes around the Central Interior produce well through the summer. Even though major hatches of chironomids, midges and mayflies are pretty much over, there are lots of opportunities to fish caddis or dragonflies through hot summer days and quiet evenings. Fly fishers who know their lakes, their habits and secrets will always be able to find willing trout. Still waters of the North Cariboo around Quesnel and Williams Lake rapidly begin to slow down during mid-July through mid-August, until they start to get the first frosts of late August that will cool them down and bring on hatches again.

Lakes up Hwy 97 north of Prince George are often at their best during the heat of summer. When northern trout have only a few short months to pack on some weight and grow a few inches, they tend to be ravenous during the emergence periods of insects. Rainbows that have been feeding on spring hatches through an often cold and wet May and June are fat and eager for surface activity, many of them 45- to 60-cm trophy fish that relish the prospect of gulping a floating caddis pattern. Look at a *Backroad* map of the country north of Summit Lake and you'll see a never-ending mass of water—huge lakes, small lakes, beaver ponds—all connected by remote and wandering creeks and rivers of the Arctic watershed. The names of the lakes are whispered by local fly fishers—Carp, Tacheeda, Hart, Freya, Boundary, Firth, Junkers and Wicheeda, wonderful waters that beckon you to visit. And best of all, most of the trout are wild stock, generated through Carp Lake origins.

Wicheeda Lake

If I were granted two days left to fish and I had to choose two places and times, a day at Wicheeda in mid-July would be my still-water choice and the Stellako River in late August my river selection.

I have difficulty writing about Wicheeda Lake, not because there is little to write about, but more the opposite. In my heart, I know that Wicheeda deserves to be protected and I hesitate to send people in there, but I also have faith that other fishers will cherish the lake as much as I do if they do go there. My hope is that perhaps if I write about Wicheeda, people

Danie Erasmus with a wild rainbow at Wicheeda Lake. Mike Quarenghi photo.

will respect and treasure it as a special fishing place—the trout are wild, the scenery spectacular, and it needs to remain so. If we work diligently to preserve Wicheeda's fragile fishery (barbless hooks, no kill limits and trail access by foot only, lake accesses untouched), this little lake will always be an extraordinary place to fish.

To access Wicheeda, bear east to the Chuchinka (700) Road from the only gas station in Bear Lake, turning left at the 704-km intersection and right at the 714-km junction. Travel east and turn onto the Wichcika FSR at about km 751, where you will drive about 4 km to the top of a hill and come to a small clearing and short 4x4 path which leads to the trailhead. It's a jaunt from Prince George, taking about three hours to get there, hike in and set up for fishing, which is why I only make the journey once or, at best, twice a year. The 700 Road is very rough gravel so I suggest a pickup truck if you plan to make the trip.

The trail is a nice fifteen-minute walk, twenty minutes if you park on top, and not rigorous; it's easy to pack a float tube or belly boat into. The lake access, however, is more difficult because the trail ends in a swampy section and can be pretty mucky and mosquito-infested but certainly bearable for the fly-fishing rewards.

Wicheeda is a shallow lake of only 3-m mean depth, maximum 7 m. It's the white marl bottom that intrigues the fly fisher—you can sight-fish trout cruising the edges, cast a fly ahead of them, and watch them come from twenty feet to intercept it—fly fishing at its best! The water is so clear you can witness the trout's frantic efforts to throw the hook and watch it torpedo off as it peels line from your reel at alarming speed.

The lake lies north and south, and is divided into two distinct sections. The first is a small bay that you are in when you come from the trail; the second and larger segment is accessed from a narrow channel on the east side of the little bay. When I fish Wicheeda I seldom need to enter the larger section, finding lots of action in the smaller one.

Wicheeda's littoral zone is staggered with random weed beds, not many of them, but enough to provide cover for trout from kingfishers, eagles and ospreys. These spots are where fish hang out during daylight hours, and they will sporadically venture into the adjacent shallows to feed and travel when insects are migrating and hatching. Find these areas and work the beds by casting to their perimeters, drawing the trout out of their cover. You only require a floating line—if conditions are right and they are on, they will charge your fly shortly after it hits the water.

My buddy Bob Graham and I made the trek into Wicheeda July 17. It was a good day for weather and fishing—clear sky, rising barometer—one of the few that we encountered in summer 2011.

It was the prime time of year for caddis to hatch, and we knew from past experiences at Wicheeda that once the sun warmed the water a little the trout would be looking for them. If they weren't active, we could create a hatch by working a dry fly over the weed beds, tantalizing feisty rainbows by skimming a caddis through the zones to make them think there was something going on.

Bingo! Wild and greedy trout came to the Mikulak caddis (see p. 97) all afternoon, ripping our fly lines into the backing, cartwheeling all over the shallow bay, creating memories for our long winter nights that will remind Bob and me once again how precious this fishery is, and how special and rewarding it is to us.

Jackson Lake

One of the prettiest little "fly fishing only" lakes in the North Cariboo, Jackson Lake (also called Jack's Hole) beckons fly fishers to its beauty every spring and summer. Not because its trout are large and plentiful, or it's a famous and adulterated fishery like Forest or Fir lakes, but for the reason that it's a special, stocked fishery, one with spectacular open scenery and camping areas, which attract fly fishers who appreciate a quiet and restful place and aren't necessarily looking for 2-kg lunkers.

Using Jackson as a base camp, a few high-quality fisheries are accessible within less than a half-hour's drive. At Elk Lake, the trout are larger but the camping is poor, and "Kestrel" Lake, an unnamed but worthy little lake, also gives up trophy trout. Jackson itself is enough to keep most fly fishers happy, the average trout creeping into the 40-cm range. It's the occasional random years of winter kills that keep it from growing exceptionally large rainbows over 50 cm.

Jackson Lake FSR Site is accessed by the Beaver Valley Road, which cuts east from McLeese Lake, thirty-five minutes north of Williams Lake and forty-five minutes south of Quesnel. Jackson Lake Road is marked, and about 18 km from Hwy 97 South at McLeese Lake. It's a slow road if you are pulling an RV or carrying a camper, but not too rough or difficult to navigate.

Jackson has an open field set for camping, plus several prime sites scattered along the lake that provide more solitude if you are lucky enough to find them empty. There's a decent boat launch suitable for a trailer, several pit toilets and a table at each site. It's a perfect Cariboo dry-fly lake, which is why it has special regulations of "fly fishing only" in place.

Jackson has superb shoals and numerous points of land, places where trout tend to congregate during intense insect hatch activity. The lake is interspersed with deep trenches, where trout can rest and wait for the inevitable migrations of nymphs, pupae and larvae of mayflies, chironomids, damselflies, dragonflies and caddis flies onto its magnificent shoals.

I have camped at Jackson many times in the past ten years—I'll always remember it as the place where my eldest son, Kevin, became addicted to fly fishing. It was late August 2003, and we were getting away for some quality time together, something we have been doing since he and his brother, Graham, were small children.

Kevin and Graham, now thirty-three and thirty-six years old, are victims of my failed first marriage. I feel it was our annual week of camping and fishing together during their formative and teenage years that kept us glued a bit—not the perfect solution, but the one that seemed to work for us. Through fishing and our mutual love of the outdoors, we found a way to connect in the short two weeks a year we had to spend together. Our love of fly fishing and the outdoors paved the way for the wonderful relationship we have now.

Kevin and I ran into what has become an annual fall ritual for me—the relentless pursuit of the water boatman flight. We fished small leeches with successes during mornings, and in early afternoons we switched to water boatmen on dry lines as they flew and splatted the lake during their daily nuptial mating flights. It was a great time to be fishing—catching twenty to thirty prime trout daily for four days, the cementing of a young adult with his father and the beginnings of what was to become a life-long hobby for Kevin, a good young man who needed a passion in life besides his work.

Fading sunlight on Forest Lake in the Cariboo. Glenn Gerbrandt photo.

Jackson has been good to me several times since. During June and July, warm summer evenings last until 10:30 p.m., prime emergence time for caddis flies as the hot sun dips below the horizon, surface water cools down and evening shadows overtake the brightness of day on Interior lakes. This is when clear-water lakes like Jackson can come alive for their best fishing of the day, their shoals no longer a menacing place for fish to linger, but a foraging zone as trout greedily search for their last meals of the day. These late-feeding fish are often the largest trout in the lake.

This last July was no exception. Arriving late with my wife, Lois, and setting camp in one of the secluded spots on the shores of Jackson, I was able to fish only an hour or two in the afternoon, picking up but one trout on a damselfly nymph. After dinner, however, when most of the fly fishers were off the lake, worn out from plying the water during the day, I fished the edges until darkness, and picked up a half-dozen trout from 40 to 50 cm on the Mikulak Traveler Sedge (see p. 97). Summer evenings are never long enough.

The East Kootenays—Endless Rivers and Creeks

If Lois and I were to pack up our possessions and move somewhere else in British Columbia, the Cranbrook–Fernie area of the East Kootenays would get my vote. Blessed with great summer weather, magnificent Rocky Mountain scenery, endless clear freestone rivers, creeks and streams and some of the most pristine lakes in BC, the East Kootenays is a fly-fishing and outdoor paradise.

This fly-fishing mecca is remotely situated in the very southeast corner of the province and, because of its distance from any major centre, remains untouched by the wrath of big city greediness. Its local flavour is interrupted only by yearly migrations of outdoor lovers—fly fishers and Alberta golfers and boaters during hot summers, and skiing enthusiasts through the short winter months. Locals profess to "being on Kootenay time," displaying a laid-back element in their lifestyles and a general gracious but carefree attitude to intervention in their lives.

Primary industries are coal mining and lumber, good-paying jobs that support the quiet lifestyles of its forty thousand people. The region

Kevin Smith holds a chunky 45-cm west slope cutthroat from a small Kootenays creek. Brian Smith photo.

encompasses about ten thousand square kilometres, with a population density of only 3.7 people per square kilometre, giving its residents lots of room to roam and enjoy the gifts of open-air life. Its major business centre is Cranbrook, with Fernie and Sparwood a hundred kilometres and an hour and a half from Cranbrook.

It's the fishing for its west slope cutthroat trout we are interested in, arguably the best the world has to offer; rivers, creeks, lakes and streams are adorned with the prettiest fish the Lord put on this planet. The Kootenays' cutthroats are the fattest trout I have ever seen, its rivers and creeks perfect factories and ideal habitats for the abundant array of insect life they produce to support the superb growth rates of their fish.

The west slope cutthroat of British Columbia is an individual species of salmonid, a strain separate from Yellowstone and coastal cutthroats. It's native to our upper Columbia River drainage and northern tributaries of Idaho's Snake River in the US. Across the Continental Divide, you'll also find them in the North Saskatchewan River and its tributaries, likewise in the headwaters of some northernmost rivers in Montana.

Their beauty is astonishing. Heavily spotted, with a greenish hue on their backs and orange-gold flanks, mature fish display pinkish bellies and strong, vibrant orange slashes beneath their jaws.

They require protection for survival, needing pristine habitats, major river systems with smaller tributaries and their branches for spawning and rearing fry, unpolluted headwaters with clean cold water, and safety from invasive hybridization of other species such as the more aggressive rainbow trout, which will devastate a cutthroat fishery within a few years if impregnated with them.

The main stem Elk River is the west slope cutthroat's home ranch, but the Elk's tributaries are their farms, places where mature trout migrate back and forth to spawn and feed. They are perfect rearing grounds for young fry, which grow hastily in these small native streams without much hindrance.

The Elk's tributaries are many, each one harbouring and nurturing its share of cutthroat populations. Their beginnings are in creeks flowing from Petain and Nivelle glaciers at the 3,000-m level in Elk Lakes Provincial Park. Upper and Lower Elk lakes are entwined by creeks and valleys, where the river begins its flow southward from Lower Elk Lake. It picks up many small creeks as it races downhill toward the town of Elkford, about 80 km south on the Elk River FSR—Tobermary, Cadorna, Abruzzi, Weary, Forsyth and Crossing creeks, to name a few. All are rich feeder streams to the Elk River system, their cutthroat fishing nothing short of spectacular in a wilderness setting few places can match.

Below Elkford, along Hwy 43 to Sparwood, a distance of 35 km, the Elk gathers major tributaries, the Fording River and Brule and Michel creeks. Below Sparwood on its journey to Fernie, several small creeks are collected—Lardner, McCool, Hosmer, Labelle, Hartley and Fairy, to name a few more. You can't overlook any of these small tributaries when fishing the Elk system, especially for a quick walk-and-wade during the evening hours after you've been in a drift boat all day. Most times, they will give you as much action as the main stem Elk, after it has filled your day with its bounties.

On its passage to Lake Koocanusa, which is about 20 km below Elko, the Elk picks up another major fly-fishing tributary, the fabled Wigwam River. Its name is spoken softly, revered among local fly fishers and tourists as one of the finest of the East Kootenays, a place where bull trout are as long as your cowboy boots and cutthroat are of equal trophy proportions. I haven't fished it, but it's rumoured that the steep access trails to reach Wigwam's rich canyon water are for the sturdy of foot and fly fishers who are part goat; not that I'm not willing to give it a go, and I will someday soon... maybe after I uncover the secrets of the mysterious Flathead River system a few valleys west of the Elk.

If drift fishing is your game, the Elk River main stem presents the visiting angler with an abundance of opportunities. Fly shops in Fernie offer guided trips from June through October, and there are several public access launch sites. The drifts my son Kevin and I have done include Fording River confluence at Line Road Bridge to Sparwood (pontoon boat best); Olson Pit Road to Hosmer; Hosmer to Fernie; and Fernie to Morrissey. Each of these drifts is from 7 to 11 km, and takes a full day to complete. There are many more put-ins along the 80-km or so route from Elkford to the Elk's terminus at Lake Koocanusa.

Tributary creeks are impossible to drift because they are too small, shallow and narrow to afford any sort of safe drifting, even with a canoe or pontoon boat. Most tribs are only a car-lane wide, and are walk-and-wade propositions. Vehicle access to get close to most them, however, is usually easy by good gravel roads, or in the case of Michel Creek, right along a paved main highway.

Elk River Main Stem

The end of July is prime time for fly fishing in the Elk River system, a week before tourists descend on the Kootenays for the August long weekend, which features long lines of Albertans scurrying across Hwy 3 through the Crowsnest Pass to their summer vacation homes, or the start of their well-deserved family boating holidays. We camp in Sparwood at Mountain Shadows Campground, smack in the middle of all the best cutty fishing the Elk system offers.

Kevin Smith "fooling" trout on the Elk River in the Kootenays.
Brian Smith photo.

My eldest son, Kevin, and I have been doing this trip for four years now, each one different than the others because rivers are unpredictable in their welcomes and flows. Sometimes water levels are up, other years they are down; occasionally, after a hot summer day, you'll find them a tad cloudy from snowmelt on the glaciers.

Unlike lake fishing, a river can be greatly affected by storms of wet weather, when a torrent of rain for several days can wipe out an otherwise settled river for a week. Ninety percent of the time the Elk is reliable during late July. If you're really unlucky and it does go out, you can usually find one of its tributaries that was unaffected by the storm, and spend a few days reliving your youth bushwhacking along one of these meandering streams deep in the mountains.

Another option in the case of an Elk blowout is to make the quick thirty-minute run into Alberta along Hwy 3, where you can fish the Crowsnest for its feisty rainbows, or the Oldman and its tributaries for more beautiful west slope cutthroats and cutt-bow hybrids. I've spent a lot of time on these streams also, literary fodder for another chapter in my books.

The put-in for the Hosmer to Fernie drift is a challenge if you're faint of heart and don't have a four-wheel-drive vehicle. The access point is the first road before the Hosmer Bridge. Turn right, take the first left for a few hundred metres and then left again to the put-in entrance above the bridge. It's a steep bank to back your drift boat down, but safe enough if you're careful. Park your trailer and vehicle at the pull-off lot beside the bridge.

This section has gorgeous water: quick gravel runs narrowing into slots and bank-lined pools, long soft glides that trout love to slip into to feed during hatches; many cutthroat-infested corner runs; and several stretches of deep, rip-rap bank water along railroad tracks that usually hold the largest trout you'll find on the Elk.

It's technical water. If you park the boat, get out and walk upstream from the main runs. You'll often find fish lying along the bank that haven't seen a fly fisher for a few days and, if you approach them carefully, they'll eagerly take your offering.

Kevin and I have found that the best way to fish the Elk is to bomb the banks with a big adult stonefly, stimulator or hopper when we're on moving drifts from pools to runs, and use small patterns like drakes, caddis flies and midges when we stop, basically matching the hatch in progress. Our most productive days are the ones we spend doing a lot of walking.

Last July was no exception—sizes 6 and 8 stonefly adults and stimulators on the drift, green drakes and caddis flies sizes 12–14 when parked. The trout were fat, feisty and strong, averaging 40 to 45 cm, a few in the 50–55-cm category, just what we have come to expect on this fabulous trout stream in the Rockies.

Michel Creek

Touted by Elk River Guiding Company in Fernie, BC, as one of North America's best walk-and-wade cutthroat fisheries, Michel Creek has seldom proven this statement wrong for us.

It's a small freestone stream with beginnings south of Hwy 3 on Michel Ridge above the 2,200-m level, where it pummels its path over 1,000 m to

50 cm cutthroat. Michel Creek, Kootenays. Brian Smith photo.

its confluence with the Elk above Sparwood. As Michel descends to the valley floor, it picks up more tiny creeks and some major tributaries, namely Leach Creek accessed along the Byron Creek Mine Road and Alexander Creek from the north side of Hwy 3. By the time Michel enters the Elk, it's about a double-lane width.

Don't let Michel Creek's size and moderate flow fool you—this is one hell of a little cutthroat stream, chock full of wild fish representing size ranges from 5-cm nursery fry to 50-cm-plus hogs, a rare size for a mature cutthroat trout that seldom reaches over 45 cm.

The best thing about Michel is its close proximity to Sparwood, the bridge at Hwy 3 only several minutes from downtown. You can drift and fish the Elk during the day, have a leisurely dinner and still catch Michel's best fishing hours from about 8 p.m. to complete darkness.

Accessed from Hwy 3, there are some public campsites scattered along the creek main stem and a few more beside the stream along the Byron Creek Mine Road, its turnoff about 10 km southeast of Sparwood.

Mountain Shadows RV Park in Sparwood offers full campsite accommodations but caters to the coal-mining crowd as well. During maintenance shutdowns in summer months this campsite can be busy, so I recommend making reservations.

When the sun goes behind Sparwood Ridge at about 8 p.m. after a hot summer day, Michel comes alive with insect hatches and returning egg-laying adults, especially caddis and drakes that have been hanging in limbo during the sweltering heat of daytime sunshine. Most evenings the emergence is so prolific and there are so many trout rising in the pools and soft runs, you have a hard time focusing on which fish to target! It's truly a glorious time to have a 3-weight rod in your hand.

Little Creeks of the Elk Main Stem

I think the Elk's little tributaries are the epitome of quiet creeks that flow from the Rockies. They offer a discerning angler the best of all we wish for when we step into the wilderness: absolute solitude (if that's what you hope for); unsurpassed mountain scenery; good exercise, wading and walking their trails; and of course, radiantly beautiful and larger than average trout to whet our fishing appetites. All of them are excellent fishing; the farther you walk, the better the action and the more remote your journey.

Small creek fishing is trout exploration at its finest. Every corner has its welcome and intriguing secrets: a fallen log, offering shade and a hiding place; a patch of large boulders, which creates feeding lanes; a long meadow with deep undercut bank, to conceal the wariest of trout; a cluster of willows, foliage that emerging insects cling to. Unlock the corners, and you'll expose the riddles of trout fishing small streams.

When creek fishing, your first cast into a run is the most important one—you must always position yourself to make it your best one, because it sets up the rest of your tactic. As I approach a run or small pool, I imagine myself the largest trout in the pod, and think "Where would I be if I were him?" and then progressively work short casts below that slot, often taking a few trout before I reach the prime holding spot. If you do take fish on the way to "Walter's" place, lead and play them downstream of the run, so you don't disturb the rest of the trout.

Fishing upstream is usually the ticket—trout face upstream, and can sense every danger, movement and disturbance from well above them, but have few inhibitions about being startled from below as long as you keep your distance and wade quietly. If you can reach runs from the bank, stay out of the water completely. Twenty-foot casts are usually adequate in small creek situations!

I have often found that tributary creeks require one size smaller fly patterns and different styles than their main stem rivers—dropping to sizes 14 and 16 and using parachute models is often a good recipe for success and positive hookups. Reduce your tippets to 5- or 6-X as well, which will allow your smaller patterns to drift more freely and tippets to be less visible on the soft currents of little streams.

These creeks have been good to me and my boys—after a few days of drifting the big river, we welcome the opportunity to do some exploring, and we are rarely disappointed. The trout are only slightly smaller than the main stem Elk, averaging 35 to 45 cm, but they make up for it in abundance, setting and tranquility. There is something about small streams that keeps you searching backroads and returning to them year after year, and the Kootenays is full of them.

The "Bugs"

Trout fishing in the Kootenays' rivers begins opening day June 15, soon after spring freshet, peaks in late July and lasts until closure October 31. It's Classified Water, including tributaries, and begins with hatches of big stoneflies: salmon flies through the month of June; golden stones early July through late August; and yellow and lime sallies appearing in late July and the first three weeks of August.

Caddis flies are the most reliable hatch, always happening, with various species coming off randomly during the day, the heaviest emergences occurring on long summer evenings throughout the entire open-water season. Most genera of river caddis flies are found in the Kootenays: Spotted Caddis, all of the time; Northern Case Maker, a very early caddis that hatches randomly throughout the season; October Caddis, late August and September; Grannom, hatching in swarms on hot August evenings; and Micro Caddis, the littlest buggers of all, which will hatch anytime.

On rivers, you don't have to get too cagey to catch trout on caddis flies because fish love them so much. I have found, however, that sizes 8 and 10 large, bushy, buoyant sedge patterns, like Mikulaks, work best during the day and you need to "match the hatch" with smaller patterns as hatches intensify during evenings.

Next up are the mayfly families: Pale Morning and Evening Duns along with the Western Green and Brown Drakes, which begin to come off in early July, peak the third and fourth weeks of July, and begin to wane by the end of August. Then you'll see Red Quills and Blue-Winged Olives (BWOs), which typically appear late August and hatch until the first frosts of late September.

Hoppers are the Elk's August and September flies when you want to drift the river. Always drop them just inches from grass-lined meadow banks—cutts are looking for them there, and will grab them in a hurry.

If I had to choose one time of year to fly fish the Kootenays, it would be late July during the peak of the Western Green Drake hatch. Most Elk River veterans plan their vacation times around this hatch, and I do too!

Nymph fishing is also productive. The usual stonefly patterns, pheasant-back mayfly larva and caddis pupae will always catch trout, but who wants to fish nymphs when you can take cutts on dry flies all day long?

Fly Patterns for Rivers and Creeks in July

If I were restricted to only five fly patterns in my boxes and the prospect of fishing rivers and creeks in July and August, what would I choose? First, I select an assortment of caddis flies. Next, I would choose an adult salmon fly (stonefly), then the green drake family, an Adams to represent the midge family, and finally a grasshopper pattern. I know I'm setting myself up for argument—my son Kevin will disagree with my choices; Graham might agree—but the caddis fly is and always will be my personal first choice for a searching pattern in any river situation, anywhere in the province, during summer months.

Why? You need to think caddis because from June through October they are always hanging around—sometimes randomly—and they are constantly available to trout in stages of larva, pupa, or my favourite, as adults. Caddis flies in some form constitute over 20 percent of a river trout's diet.

Stoneflies are my second choice because of their enormous size and also because I like to use them when drift fishing from a boat. It's hard to be without them, but in reality they hatch only sporadically for most of the year, the heaviest hatches occurring during high-water periods of late June and early July.

Even though mayflies are a river trout's main diet in some form and are always on the menu because of inherent availability, they are small potatoes compared to caddis flies. The green drake family is one exception. For a few weeks in the summer, they are the best patterns in your fly box.

Midges? What can I say? They surely are important, likely a larger percentage of a river trout's diet than caddis. From my personal perspective, I know trout gorge on them, but I think fish find caddis more interesting than midges. My choice of the Adams would be sizes 18–22, using the parachute form for sizes 20 and 22, which would also satisfy the need for a tiny Blue-Winged Olive mayfly if need be.

Hoppers fall into my August and September fly selection for drifting from a boat, searching banks and meadows, and general looking-for-fish activity.

Caddis Fly: For Rivers and Creeks

Just like still-water fishing with caddis flies, rivers have their own breeds of the insect. Some are the same, like the big travellers, but most are smaller varieties such as Spotted Caddis, Northern Case Maker, Grannom and Micro Caddis. The exception is the October Caddis, which is cinnamon-orange in colour, up to 30 mm in length, and begins to emerge in moving waters during August, lasting through October. It's a productive searching pattern to use late in the year when there is little insect activity around your favourite stream.

River caddis flies also have larva and pupa stages, but we're talking about favourite patterns here, so to keep the list short I'm partial to dry-fly fishing over nymphing techniques, and I'll forsake the larva and pupa stages, which I've covered under the caddis still-water section of this book in chapter 4.

For dry-fly caddis fishing, my favourite pattern by far, which accounts for probably 50 percent of my success in rivers, is the Spotted Caddis. They can be small, less than 10 mm in length, but most commonly found in a comfortable size range of 15 mm, about a size 12 or 14 Tiemco 2312. I use my standard Mikulak Traveler Sedge pattern (see p. 97) to represent the smaller Spotted Caddis.

When fishing is slow and there is no hatching activity present, I'll frequently resort to a size 8 or 10 Mikulak, normally a lake model, and skitter them around a river, often stirring the wariest of trout from their lairs.

There are also times when I have to go smaller, not to the extent of size 20 Micro Caddis, but sizes 16 and 18, for which I tie an emerging style of caddis adapted from early standby patterns of the Elk Hair Caddis imitation (see p. 101).

Rob Bryce with a good-sized Dolly Varden at Anzac River. Erich Franz photo.

Stoneflies: "Romancing the Stone"

Big, bold and cumbersome, giant stoneflies emerging from a wilderness river or returning to the water to eject their young nymphs provoke feeding responses from trout that no other insect can duplicate. They skitter, stumble and scurry across rivers. Because they're the largest food item in the water, trout can't be blamed for losing all sense of caution when stoneflies begin to perform.

Skwalas are first to awaken. If you fish southern rivers in early spring, you will notice them as early as March, but in northern waters they tend to emerge along with the larger salmon flies, first appearing during the full moon of high water in June. Lastly there are the Golden Stoneflies, fair princes and maidens of summer months, and along with them the Little Yellows and Little Olives that also grace our rivers during July and August.

Identification of stoneflies is by colour markings: Skwalas have drab olive bodies, very dark wings and yellow head highlights; salmon flies have orange-brown bodies, dark wings and orange head colourations; Golden Stones have brown bodies, light wings and golden yellow head distinctions.

In my younger days before I became hooked on fishing the dry fly, I angled the nymph stage a lot, using them as my go-to searching patterns in rivers like the Blackwater and Stellako. They produced a lot of trout for me, and still would today if I put them in the water, but I find the nymph phase is passé compared to the robust action generated by the adult stage. But I will fish them if I have to.

I think stoneflies or imitations of them, all of the rubber-legged and hairy-looking things fly tiers design and throw at trout, are the most-fished and versatile patterns for fly fishers who love to drift and cast a dry fly when on the move in a boat. I haven't confirmed this by speaking to a lot of guides, but I'll wager a bet gillies will suggest a stimulator or stonefly to their clients 80 percent of the time when asked for a recommendation for a drift pattern.

How long will my love affair with stoneflies last? Hopefully as long as I can wade and fish.

Julian Franz landing grayling at Anzac River, north of Prince George.
Erich Franz photo.

Drakes: Irresistible Mayflies

When the drake families begin to show during July, after high water and some hot days to bring the river temperature up a little, trout become very selective to them. The emergence of Green and Brown Drakes, Flavilinea

(Flavs) and Slate-Winged Olives (SWOs) signals the best fishing of the summer months, stirring anglers from all over North America to head for their favourite Rocky Mountain streams to test their skills against cutthroat and rainbow trout.

Sporadic hatches of stoneflies are still around and will still fool trout. Caddis flies are relegated to evening propositions, because when the drakes begin to appear, trout will key on them. Drakes must taste good to big trout. Because they seldom hatch in mass numbers, they are elusive enough to send even the largest fish in the run into soft water during midday to search for random drake morsels coming off the water.

The drake families hatch together. Often you'll see some of each coming off in irregular unison, always in the quiet water of runs, or in the side channels and back eddies of quick currents. It is riffle water they preferred as nymphs, greens and SWOs clinging under rocks and debris, browns burrowing into silt, gravel and mud. But when emergence beckons, it's off to the easy water they go, crawling, tumbling and drifting into an unknown season of adulthood—at last at the mercy of the marauding and happy trout.

Green Drakes and Flavs are easy prey for trout. They emerge slowly, often riding a current for 50 m or so as they transform to the dun stage on top of the water, and take great painful (it must seem to them) seconds to dry their wings and vacate the premises. Trout have seen this act before and relish the moment, taking trapped adults in slow motion and big slurps as the duns struggle to become airborne.

Brown Drakes are better suited—they are the biggest and strongest of the lot, and can emerge under water, popping through the surface film and becoming air traffic immediately. I've tried on many occasions to capture a camera shot of an emerging brown to no avail; they are up, off and out of sight in a fleeting instant of glory. This is an important detail to the fly fisher—even though brown drakes seem to be on the menu, you may have better chances with a green model!

August: Summer Wanes

For a fly fisher living in the northern reaches of British Columbia, August is a time of yearning. We enter the month full of enthusiasm and finish it with a longing for the optimism that spring always brings: warm days, a full fishing season ahead, fresh adventures, new patterns to try and a full fly box. Our lingering hope for August is that we are leaving the lakes and streams without regrets, and that we'll live through another northern winter to fish once again next spring.

August is the beginning of the fishing year's end—two months hence we'll expect our first look at winter with snow on the hills. Perhaps it won't stay, but it often does. Hummingbirds have forsaken us for their long journeys back to South America with their young. Robins have begun to gather their migration flocks; Canada geese are gathering for their southward journeys down north-south valleys from their summer breeding grounds in the far north. It's time to mourn the summer's passing, but also a season to reflect on our amazing natural surroundings.

It's also wild harvest time, as our tables and freezers are enriched with an abundance of ripening berry crops—mountain blueberries, saskatoons, huckleberries, currants, gooseberries, cranberries and raspberries—their seasons also ending, maturing for picking before the first frosts later in the

BJ Bruder (née Smith) with a nice 45-cm trout at Scuitto Lake, Kamloops area. Aaron Bruder photo.

month. Wild fowl is in consumption mode, greedily feasting on the rich banquet, readying their bodies for a long winter ahead.

It's not that August is a dismal month for northern people—days have average highs of 21°C and lows of 7°C, but those warm summer days are usually clustered into the beginning of the month. By the end of August, we'll wake up to cold mornings and heavy dew or frost on our truck wind-shields, certain signs of impending fall weather. If you're camping in the back country, late August means warm clothing around the campfire at night and again for morning breakfasts, but into shorts by noon. And, if you're an avid steelhead fly fisher (I'll do it, but I don't live for it), it's the beginning of your favourite fishing season.

There is no question that August can be a tough time for fishing Interior lakes. The big hatches of chironomids, mayflies, damsels and caddis flies have ended, and water temperatures are the warmest of the year, usually above the 13–15°C that trout favour, forcing most lakes into the period we call "summer doldrums."

You've heard that old baseball term, "the dog days of August." In baseball, it's been a busy spring on the diamond, preening players, tweaking lineups and playing through injuries. August is about hurt and tired arms and legs, sometimes lazy attitudes and, if you're out of the pennant race, it's about next year. The best and strongest teams make their runs to the pennant in August.

Lakes are no different—they can only produce what their compositions and climates will allow, then they need a rest. Depending on elevation, lakes turn off in late July and back on in late August when a week of cool nights forces a drop in water temperature. High-country North Cariboo lakes like Jackson, Forest, Marmot and Fir, plus all of the lakes north of Prince George, will begin to see water boatman activity during the last week of August. You'll want to catch this hatch early on, because after a few weeks of dining on the hard exoskeletons of water boatmen and backswimmers, trout get weary of working to digest them, and will go off their diets completely for a week or two. If trout are actively showing on the surface, they will still attack a floating caddis fly. Staple fly patterns, however, like leeches, dragonfly nymphs and scuds, most presented deeply with sinking fly lines, will be your best producers.

In great rivers of the northwest, salmon and steelhead summer migrations reach their peaks in early August and wane for the rest of the month. Their tributary waters, however, are just beginning to feel the rush of their fishes' adrenaline, as abundant salmonids press onward upriver in their quest to spawn and deliver themselves onto perfect gravel beds in their native streams. It's a ritual etched in time: the return of mature fish, which several years before were alevins, arriving once more at their home waters, back from their feeding grounds in the mysterious Pacific Ocean where they gorged on plankton and crustaceans, the rich marine environment growing them to magnificent proportions. The salmon will spawn and die, but the strongest steelheads will recoup and return to the sea, the most robust fish sometimes returning for several spawns.

Skeena River is at its best during the first weeks of August. Sockeye salmon and steelhead are moving through in vast numbers, and a few weeks behind them, cohos. Many of my friends are filling their coolers with fly-caught (although many are "flossed") sockeye, the best eating of all salmon. If you have access to a seaworthy boat, a journey down the Douglas Channel for coho and spring salmon makes a wonderful vacation. Within a month, it will be prime time for a steelhead trip to the Bulkley and Morice rivers.

The seemingly endless hatches of insects on trout rivers begins to subside during late August, but fishing pressure has also dwindled, and it's one of my favourite times of year to walk and wade trout streams. Heavy spring flows have diminished, exposing boulders that enhance pocket water, the places where feeding trout love to lie. Fast, unruly runs and glides that were not approachable during June and July give up their slots and ledges, and can once more be navigated and fished easily without fear of dunking. River crossings are safer. Trout are wary, although easier to find.

Fishing Places

August is a time of deep contemplation and, for me, a desperate rush to plan and complete the goals of my fishing season. If you are a serious fly fisher, I think you need to set goals and objectives during the preceding winter, aims that will satisfy the needs of everyone important to you—wife, children, family, friends and, most essentially, yourself.

As years pile up on us we must face the inevitable prospects of our declining health, and too often must deal with the agony of cherished friends and relatives passing. Our bodies give us an allotment of miles; some get more, but far too many receive less than their share. Our early adulthood is usually spent giving a whole lot more than getting: raising children, paying bills and trying to save for our "golden" years, a period in our lives each of us addicted "old" fly fishers hopes and dreams will be duly rationed in our personal favour.

I have lost some fishing friends during the past few years: Bob Jones, a fine author/editor, whom I credit with giving me the "itch" to write; Bob Melrose, one of the finest fly fishers and teachers of the sport the north will ever see; Jim Mills, a close and dear friend from my youth who taught me much about fishing, and usually out-fished me; Sheldon Moore, often outspoken, but seldom out-fished; and Dan Cassavant, a "gilly" who came home. I know in my heart if they had one more week to live and one wish for it, a few days' fishing with old friends would be foremost on the short list. I wish I had given more of my time to them.

Rivers continue to possess me during August. In the north, the Stellako, Bowron, Willow, McLeod and everything around them are at their best. In the North Cariboo and Chilcotin, the Blackwater, Canim, Horsefly, upper Dean and tributaries are in perfect summer condition and I'll try to get at them as much as I can. Rivers and streams draining the west and east slopes of the Rocky Mountains into the Kootenays and Alberta are also in favour with the wandering fly fisher, as the last hatches of green drakes will bring the most discerning cutthroats to the surface. Hopper flights and sporadic late-season hatches of midges and terrestrials will once again bring glory to our fly-fishing days.

Terrestrials are a key part of the trout diet in late summer. In rivers, the drying of meadow grasses and hot winds of early August will spur the flights of grasshoppers, a favourite meal for trout, and fish line up along the banks of every field to clobber the struggling insects as they valiantly try to recover from their swimming ordeals. Ants hatch and fly forth to form new colonies; beetles and bugs meet their fate as they drop from trees and foliage into an unforgiving trout stream.

Douglas Channel, Kitimat

Late August is a special time for my wife, Lois, me and two of our closest friends. For the past four or five years, it's been a ritual to join our good friends Jim Lewis and his partner, Vivian Cameron, for a week or so on their boat, *Spikim*, when we will venture down Douglas Channel from Kitimat to fish, crab, prawn and generally veg out for a week.

Jim and I grew up, went to school and played sports together in White Rock, and have a friendship that has lasted over forty-five years. We drifted apart for thirty years, each marrying and raising our children, living in different parts of the province, but we always kept in touch at Christmas. When Jim's son Mike moved to Terrace to purchase and operate his hunting and guiding business, Jim soon followed, invested in a sturdy trawler-style

Coho Salmon—Freight Trains on the Fly

Among the salmon, cohos are the most sought after for the fly fisher. Unlike sockeye, which feed and strike lures sporadically or not at all during their migrations, cohos are a game fish; they will charge 10 m across a beach or pool to intercept a fly if so inclined. On long gravel-lined shorelines and in ocean channels and estuaries, as they herd in schools along their paths to home rivers, cohos feed ravenously and are a favourite target for fly fishers. Beach and estuary patterns commonly used are muddlers and tinsel-bodied flies in red, orange, yellow and pink; in the channels, bucktail flies accented in blue, olive green and pink with white polar bear crests representing herring, anchovies, squid or shrimp can be trolled with a fly line in the wake of your boat with astonishing success. If you have never caught a coho in salt water with a fly rod, it must be put on your bucket list.

Cohos spawn in fresh water, travelling to the upper reaches of their home stream's tiniest tributaries, their eggs hatching in late winter after about two months in redds. The little alevins remain hidden in the gravel for another one to two months, living on and absorbing their yolk sacs. Once the egg sacs are devoured, the fry escape the gravel and begin their search for food, remaining in their natal streams for one to two years. After their transformation from parr-marked fry into smolts of 10–15-cm lengths, they flush to the ocean for the remainder of their lives, returning to their birthplaces in one to three years to spawn and die.

Sadly, coho is one salmon adversely affected by logging, irrigation and damming practices, not so much in the northwest as most of our creeks and rivers are freestone and not dammed, but in coastal areas where water control has damaged much of its habitat. Coho will search for the uppermost reaches of natal streams to spawn, commonly doing so in the shallow water of gravel-lined creeks (or even in ditches that were once creeks), water that will barely cover their backs. If disturbed, logged to riverbed, silted by mud or foolishly diverted, these altered rivulets are their deathbeds, for the young salmon cannot free themselves, breathe or escape from the damaged, captive creeks. They are, however, resilient fish, and their stocks can be restored quite easily if their habitat is improved and respected.

Sunset fades on Kildala Arm, Douglas Channel, Kitimat. Brian Smith photo.

boat that he moors at Kitimat, and the rest is our new history. Our friendship has rekindled, and our paths will always be united. Jim and Vivian are like brother and sister to us.

The BC coastline is a magnificent piece of the world. The farther north you go, the more remote your experiences: endless mountain and sea vistas, the mountains' feet disappearing hundreds of metres to the depths of the ocean floor; majestic, deep, sweeping valleys, each with river or creek converging on channel inlets and arms; desolate, moonlit and starry evenings, with only the lapping of waves and friends your company. It's quite an awakening to be isolated on water for five days and nights, seldom leaving the boat, to see nothing but mountains meeting water, rarely another boat or soul, to moor in secluded coves, rising and falling with the tides.

We go to fish, but not feverishly. We take what comes, as you must when you fish the ever-changing waters of ocean tides. Sometimes the salmon run is in your favour, the schools having turned to your side of the channel, but often they're not, and are concentrated many kilometres away from you, and you don't know where. Your boat runs slowly, about seven knots top speed, so you can't overtake or chase the runs; they must come to you. You must guess correctly to cross their paths. But there are always crabs and prawns, feasts fit for kings and their queens, the traps dropped at night and gathered in morning, their heavy cages laden with the evening's dinner.

The downriggers are out the sides, hoochies or cut herring on the deeply trolled lines and heavy rods, and my 9-weight fly rod with bucktail fly runs out the middle, trolling 10–15 m behind the boat in its wake. Our purpose is set—we are on the hunt, looking for coho or perhaps a random late-running spring salmon, our watercraft criss-crossing the arms and inlets, turning corners, looking for current lines, rip tides and kelp beds where food gathers, and the salmon that slash through them in their feeding frenzy.

The ledge is shallow, only 10 m deep, but the salmon have gathered on it and, on this day, we too have found it. The strike is explosive, my vintage Hardy reel overcome with joy, singing loudly as the prime coho takes his first frantic run and peels several hundred yards of fly line and backing from my reel. He's big and strong, and on we go for twenty minutes, the fish charging and circling the boat at will, sometimes winning ground on the light rod, often losing it, but fighting until exhausted. Finally, he succumbs, turns to his side and welcomes the net. He's a fine coho: perhaps 7 kg, silver, fat and strong, my first on a buck tailfly—one to cherish, and the first of more in years to come.

We treasure this time together, our friends and us, living, laughing, eating well and reminiscing, brought together again by a common love for the boat, water and fishing.

The Stellako—I Return

When I return to the Stellako after a few months' absence, it's becoming more and more like an old friend to me—predictable and reliable, like a pair of well-worn shoes. I'm not in a hurry to get my rod in the water, preferring rather to linger a while at the bridge, watch the river move, study the flow and drink of my experience, because I know that even if I am treated unkindly (which means a skunk plus a dunking), it's one of the finest rivers in North America, and a privilege to be near it once again.

To quantify that statement, I realize there are many wild trout rivers on our continent that will give up 60-cm resident rainbows, but most are remote fly-in experiences, exclusive to wealthy fly fishers who aren't cost-conscious, which rules out me and 95 percent of the world's population. You can fish the Stellako for a week with double occupancy, stay in a cabin at Stellako Lodge, close enough to the river that you can roll into it off the cabin's verandas, and spend as little as $500 plus groceries for the experience. This you cannot do in most countries of the world!

The reason the Stellako remains a trophy wild trout fishery is because of its access—easy to get to at its outlet by paved roads, but not accessible by road below the bridge for its 11-km length. The only way to get downriver is by a few rough trails or watercraft, which leaves the middle sections of the Stellako lightly fished, highly productive and its trout less wary.

Bob Graham at the "rock garden" run. Stellako River. Brian Smith photo.

It's also Class 3–4 water with a portage around two unnavigable drops, not a stream for the novice river runner. You need a reliable pontoon boat or rubber raft with a top quality bottom fabric that will take the abuse of the occasional bottom rub without damaging the denier. An experienced canoeist can navigate the Stellako as well, but I've seen the carnage of wrecks along its banks almost every time I venture down.

The rough trail along the Stellako's south bank accesses the cabin pool, about 1 km below the bridge. Below the cabin run, the trail was victim to the infamous ice storm of winter 2006. The trail now sports deadfalls and wader-rippers galore through this stretch, which has since limited fly-fishing access to the lower river. The hike to more great water downriver can be accomplished by wading along the south bank. Few of us "old guys," however, are energetic and young enough to tackle 2–3 km of really tough slugging (more so getting back upriver!) to venture downstream. Besides, there are lots of fish in the top 2 km—you just have to be a little cagey to catch them!

Below the Glenannan Bridge at the outlet, the river is fly fishing only from the 1- to 5-km markers; I have rarely seen, however, any angler using other than flies in the Stellako. Some of the hike-in spots are poached occasionally, which is shameful but not unexpected for a trophy river. For the most part, the Stellako is fished by diehard fans who have been visiting annually for thirty years or more—northerners like me who have fallen madly in love with the river—a few local fly fishers, and the odd curious "south of 52nd parallel" fly fisher. It takes a few years of toil to learn her secrets, but these are the challenges of our sport: patience, willingness, worthiness and always the possibility of seducing a 60-cm wild resident rainbow.

Some people say July is the best time to fish the Stellako. I agree from an insect-hatch point of view, but August is my favourite and close behind is early to mid-September, before the height of the annual run of sockeye salmon, and when river flows have diminished. I'll return to the river in October, when there is little hope of raising a trout to a dry fly, and I'll target trout that follow the sockeyes on their routes upriver—it will be a fine climax to my fishing year.

The population and health of the Stellako's resident trout fishery fluctuates with the four-year cycle of returning sockeyes to the river. In years of abundance, every fourth year, the trout population can swell to several thousand, diminishing progressively until the "big" rotation returns. Disruptions in the salmon migrations (environment, disaster, interference) can greatly influence the health of the short river and its flows, hence the populace of its resident rainbows.

The theory, substantiated by snorkel count surveys according to Ray Pillipow, a fisheries biologist in the Omineca Region, is that the river contains a five-year average of about five thousand resident trout in size ranges of 10 to 60 cm. Sixty percent (3,000) are between 30 to 50 cm; of this number, it's estimated 20 percent (600) are mature trout over 45 cm; of that number, about 15 percent (90) are 50 cm and larger. Fisheries counts and research indicates that 90 percent of the resident rainbow populace lives above the falls, or in the upper 7 km of river.

The Stellako is a fertile river, especially at the top end, where its flow and temperature is moderated by Francois Lake, one of the largest in the Lakes District at 110 km long. My estimate is mayfly species comprise about 40 percent of the hatches, caddis flies another 40 percent and stoneflies about 20 percent. During August, mayfly hatches are slowing down a little and adult stoneflies are seen very randomly, but caddis flies are regular contributors to the flurry of evening insect activities with huge hatches of Grannoms. Northern Case Makers (cinnamon caddis) and Spotted Caddis provide plenty of daytime hatching commotion.

Rusty orange, whether it's a body, wing or trailing shuck, is a colour that seems to send the rainbows of the Stellako nuts, and should be a part of your fly pattern selections for late-summer fishing in the river. My Grannom and cinnamon caddis patterns are personal favourites for August (see p. 107).

It's the second week of August 2010. The river has dropped into what I call perfect condition for my "getting older" pair of legs—moderate flow, thigh-deep height at the bridge runs and just warm enough for swimming at the lake's outlet, likely about 15–18°C. Saskatoon berries, outrageously abundant at the Stellako, are fully ripe and deliciously sweet owing to our usual berry-perfect northern summer weather conditions of moderate rainfalls and warm, dry days. We've rented cabin Number 2 again for a week's stay, surrounded by familiar friends, Uwe and Lois Ihssen from Campbell River, BC, and Joel and Martine Sarkissian from Lyon, France.

It's the third reunion for Lois and me with these wonderful friends with whom the Stellako has rewarded us, two couples from far away who have found the river offers everything they can ask for in a vacation.

When we fish together, Uwe can always be found on the river at 6:30 a.m., early for my liking, the water cool and often shrouded in mist of first light, rays of sun struggling to burn through a fading haze. Joel is not far behind, fishing "his" run on the opposite south bank from Uwe, quietly but resolutely plying the water for his first trout of the day. I linger on the bridge, un-wadered with black coffee in hand, watching my friends as they taste the experience in the increasing brightness of early morning on our river of hope, camera always ready for a perfect photo.

It doesn't take many Stellako trout to make memories—one pull per day is enough if you can survive the slash of a 45–60-cm rainbow on 5-X tippet using a size #14–22 dry fly! Some days, for a short hour or two when conditions are right—subdued light, hatch in progress, and rising barometer—the river comes alive with feeding trout. Most are immature, in the 25–35-cm range; larger ones are hunkered in their lies on clefts of ledges or behind boulders waiting for the flawless drift of a nymph or skitter of an emerging insect. The trophy trout eat surface flies with reluctance during the day in the bridge runs, preferring to lose their inhibitions with the fading light of evenings, or during a sudden rain squall at midday—best to be ready when they are!

Uwe prompts a slashing rise and take for his first fish of the day, followed by his familiar holler of "Hoh!" which signifies his worthy triumph—it's a fine trout of 45 cm, vividly marked with dark crimson lateral band, heavily spotted flanks and tail and back of dark olive green—a mature resident rainbow.

Not to be outdone, Joel entices a larger trout from his run on the opposite bank to sip a small adult caddis that he is fluttering under the surface. His fish is easily 50 cm, taken from the depression of a soft run that snorkellers say holds the largest residents of the bridge runs.

Our trout seem to like the dim light the fog has cast on the scene. Soon the lengthening sun, beginning to gather strength and vigour, will burn the mist from the river and its trophy fish will once again slip into their hideaways to remain camouflaged, unseen, and to feed on nymphs, awaiting another perfect time to rise and eat the river's surface insects. It will come, but not now... my friends have taken of the moment, and are content to just be in it.

After a hearty breakfast that will carry me for the day, I head downriver alone to fish favourite pools and glides below the cabin. At the bridge the previous evening, the caddis hatch of dark Grannoms was spectacular. Today, many females will return to the river mated, and will deposit their eggs in slow currents and riffles, the start of next year's generation. It's an act I'm ready for—more emerging caddis during the day and an evening episode of egg-laying returnees.

Creating the hatch began slowly. Many casts were perfectly placed over trout-laden runs before the sun crept over the hill that shadowed the river, warming my back and coaxing a few caddis to flee from their shucks and flutter over the stream's surface. Trout began to rise, first one, then another, and more—soon it was a frenzy and the river was alive with willing trout. My Grannom caddis emerger (see p. 107) worked perfectly, a little reluctantly at first, but soon had lured many fine trout to 50 cm.

This week in August was the first of many similar days on the river: seclusion, random hatches, eager trout and the good company of old friends—a perfect recipe for memories.

The Blackwater (West Road) River—Another of God's Finest

The Blackwater is another special place for me, and where my love for wilderness rivers of the Central Interior began twenty-odd years ago. It's a secluded stream that most ardent BC fly fishers have heard about, talk about visiting and want to come, but seldom visit.

The river begins high in the Chilcotin, starting its life as a maze of trickling creeks in a remote valley separating the Ilgachuz and Itcha mountain ranges, flowing not south and west to the sea, but north and east to the Fraser and then south. Along its 320-km length, it gathers momentum and increasing current from more remote tributaries—the Kushya, Euchiniko, Nazko, and Baezaeko rivers and all their branches. It spills into and runs through a series of wilderness lakes whose names are synonymous with the Carrier First Nation's tradition: Eliguk, Tsacha, Kluskus, Euchiniko and Kluskoil lakes.

Brian Smith seeking trout on the Blackwater River. Graham Smith photo.

It's a wilderness lover's paradise, endowed with tales of Native lore and of the legendary pioneer cattle ranching exploits of Rich Hobson and Pan Phillips during the Great Depression, and their struggles and triumphs against formidable odds to build the Commonwealth's largest cattle ranch of the World War II era.

Fishing is spectacular in Blackwater country. The fertile, boggy meadows of the upper valleys exude nutrients that leach into the Blackwater's tributaries, which foster voluminous hordes of insect life, creating a stream rich in abundance for building and maintaining its fish population. The river is self-sustaining and unchecked, supporting many species of fish: the Blackwater strain of wild rainbow trout; enormous and cannibalistic Dolly Varden trout; northern pike minnows; whitefishes; chinook salmon; and finally, a small run of summer-run steelheads.

It's remote fishing country, with only three bridge access points that you would judge easy to get at. The rest is ATV and rough forest service

Chinee Falls, Blackwater River. Richard Barrie photo.

fire access trails, which in early years could be traversed only by horse. The river's isolation is yet another reason for its remarkable fishing, and why people who do fish it regularly are stamped with an indelible impression of its fishing and wildlife bounties.

Blackwater rainbows become genetically cannibalistic at a young age by learning to feed voraciously on the river's healthy smorgasbord of coarse fish, and have become a valuable stocking resource for our province's fisheries program in that they will keep a freshwater lake in balance if introduced to water that has an abundance of coarse fish. True to their river upbringing, Blackwater trout are shallow-water feeders, and are at home in a lake environment that has extensive shoal areas and not great depths. Dragon Lake in Quesnel is a perfect example of Blackwater trout at work, although Dragon is void of coarse fish.

Blackwater trout are not large, averaging 30–40 cm, but aggressive, strong and willing to rise for high-floating dry flies. They prefer quicker

Four Days on the Blackwater River

My boys, Kevin and Graham, have loved the Blackwater since they were sixteen and fourteen years old. When they were much younger, we mostly fished lakes, and they learned the habits of trout, and adoration for simple things in life that are free, away from encumbrances of everyday life that teenagers seemed to get bogged down with. They learned to catch fish with flies at the early ages of four and two and the curiosity crept into them innocently, eventually becoming a passion for them that they cannot forsake. It's how we vacation together today, and how we probably will for the rest of our time together.

We have spent many too-short days together on the Blackwater. It's a perfect river to teach children the art of fly fishing—the trout come easily for flies whether they are presented well or poorly, and casts are not required to be long and graceful—often the fish lie within twenty feet of your rod tip. And the trout are not large and difficult to handle, but rise freely to jump and run with panic when hooked.

In late August 2009, Graham and I took some time and our pontoon boats to explore some of the river's infrequently fished sections. In particular, we wished to discover the Baezaeko River run from the put-in, down to the Blackwater, and then on to the West Road FS Campsite at Nazko Bridge where we had pitched our tents—about 10 km of river. Another float we wanted to do was one of my favourites, the Gillies Crossing to Batnuni Bridge run, featuring superb pocket water, a canyon portage and some butt-puckering Class 4 rapids.

The Baezaeko River put-in is an interesting spot to find. It's in the *Chilcotin Backroad Mapbook*, but that's about as much help as you're going to get. Take the first logging road south of Nazko campsite, stay on the main road, avoiding any offshoot trails (I took most of them), and you'll come to an old homestead entrance after about 4 km. Turn right onto the bush road at this spot and you'll come to the bridge put-in after about 1 km.

The Baezaeko is a major tributary about half the size of the Blackwater. In late August it is quite low and barely navigable for pontoon boats on the 2-km run down to its merging with the Blackwater.

We expected decent trout fishing in the Baezaeko, but didn't find the pools and soft corner water we were anticipating in this section of river—it's really a shotgun race downriver to the Blackwater. If I were targeting the Baezaeko fishery, I would make a few days of it, take a tent and supplies, perhaps a canoe, and choose the put-in at the bridge off the Coglistiko (4000 Road), which looks like a 50-km wilderness journey downriver to the Nazko Bridge. Of course, you'll have to get back to your parked vehicle afterwards, so you'll require two vehicles to make the trip.

Fly fishing was excellent at the merging of the Baezaeko with the Blackwater. The rest of the trip downriver was as expected—good but not great—as I had fished this section many times in the past from the opposite side of the river, which has an ATV or short-wheelbase 4x4 access trail.

The Gillies Crossing to Batnuni Bridge run was such a treat we did it twice over the next two days. This is my favourite section of the Blackwater below Nazko Road, sporting what I think is the best pocket and rock-pile water on its lower sections. You should fish this section with a buddy, take an extra oar, and be prepared to portage around the last passage of Class 4 lower canyon water, a short but unnerving and narrow piece of fast water that has capsized many unknowing rafters.

We caught many trout, thirty to forty per day, most of them falling prey to my Salmon Fly pattern (see p. 103), but also to hoppers floated through pocket water behind rocks, back eddy pools and soft side water of quick chutes.

I yearn to fish the upper sections of the Blackwater, where I know trout are larger, the river is wilder, people are fewer and its skies are painted with more brilliant sunsets. The river beckons me to its limits and I want more.

sections of river, where there are boulders and pocket water to hide in, and stretches where the river narrows into fast chutes and invariably forms back eddies that trap and concentrate their food sources. Very seldom will you find these trout in abundance through soft sections of slow-moving meadow water, but always on the many corners of the meandering river that push against a bank to create diversions.

One of the most prolific hatches in the river is salmon flies, coming off the Blackwater in mid-June coinciding with opening day, but it's also one of the hardest hatches to key on, because the river is normally high until mid-July. I've caught the major emergence only once, opening day in 2004, when we had an unusually low snowpack from the previous winter, runoff was light, and the river was in prime shape a month early. It was a glorious day, the trout were wonderfully cooperative, and I lost count of the ones I released after fifty!

Blackwater trout are not hook shy; neither are they brilliant from being caught a few times, because the river receives little pressure. Nor do they care about what time of year it is, or what is *supposed* to be happening. I've used my Stonefly Adult, Salmon Fly imitation (see p. 103) through the entire fishing season from June to September on the Blackwater; it's one of my favourite searching patterns for any river I fish.

Other favourite patterns for the Blackwater in August are caddis fly and mayfly imitations. Both genera come off the river in hordes during the summer, caddis flies the hottest item during the evening, mayflies in the day, usually in a sombre grey-toned colour. For a caddis fly, my choice on the Blackwater is the Caddis Adult, Spotted #14 (see p. 101). For a mayfly, I like an Adams #16–20 (see p. 95), size depending on what is happening. As I said, these fish are not fussy about your fly as long as it floats. I have never seen a prolific hatch of green or brown drakes on the Blackwater.

Still-water Lakes

In still-water lakes, with long northern summer days shortening into the stillness of windless autumn splendour, insect activity has slowed to a crawl, literally, and your best bet to pick up a few fish is to resort to basics of the insect orders, mostly wet patterns fished above the thermocline with sinking fly lines: dragonfly nymphs, scuds and leeches.

Trout don't come easily at this time of year, often only feeding for short bursts of a favourable solunar period, or during evenings. It's all about water temperature and where the thermocline marks the layering of a lake. As summer sets in, the upper strata of lakes receive heat from the blistering sun, which can only penetrate into the lake 5 m or so. Spring winds have lessened, which causes less mixing of the water column, and lakes form a layer of oxygen-deprived colder water. The boundary between the layers is called the "thermocline."

Trout prefer to live above the thermocline, but this warmer layer of water is also oxygen poor, hence they become lethargic and don't feed aggressively or eat the flies with the same vigour they showed in spring and early summer. When the hot sun drops below the horizon and the air temperature begins to fall, these sluggish trout will slink to the shoals for their daily feeding routines, which is why there is a flurry of activity just before nightfall on most Interior lakes, and often through the darkness of evening. This is the time to use Mikulak sedges once more, dropping them around the weed beds, usually for your best trout fishing of the day.

If you fish high-country Cariboo lakes you can often outwit the seasons, because summer doldrums don't last very long, seldom more than a few weeks. In low-elevation lakes like Dragon, it can last for six to eight weeks.

You can use the same popular patterns in August that you used in spring and early summer: Darner Dragonfly Nymphs (see p. 100), Gammarus Shrimps (see p. 85) and Blood Bugger Leeches (see p. 86). You should, however, use smaller imitations, dropping your fly a couple of sizes, because the dominant insects crawling and swimming will be immature young and will be under-sized compared to adults, which prevailed earlier in the year. Size matters! Mikulaks in sizes 8 and 10 skittered on the shoals through 1–2 m of water will surely interest the wariest of foe, and you'll be glad you thought of it.

Water boatman patterns are another late-August favourite for me, but I'll save it for the insect's prime month of September.

Creeks and Rivers

How can a serious fly fisher resist a river in August? As Roderick Haig-Brown wrote in *Fisherman's Summer*, "summer days are golden days and for me summer streams are golden streams. I love the freedom from bulky clothing, the feel of cool water against my waders..." Oh, how those words conjure a warm feeling in my soul when I read them!

In northern waters, August invariably comes in hot and goes out cooler, and with the onset of chilly nights insect hatches dwindle to a sparse few, but what is there is worthwhile for the ardent fly fisher. Caddis remain a notable item on a trout's dinner menu, but small ones like Grannoms, the exception being the initial emergences of good-sized October Caddis on some rivers and streams. Hoppers are the wake-up fly of choice, fished within inches of grass-lined banks and back eddy entrapments; you should, however, not overlook angling with other late-summer terrestrials that trout relish, and that actually comprise more of a trout's fall diet than do hoppers—ants, beetles and crane flies.

Trout are easier to find as river levels drop, but fish are more wary of intruders than during high-water months. Great stealth is in order, and you quickly learn that by splashing and cajoling through your river at break-neck speed catchable trout are scattering in front of you like water spiders. It's another learning curve in the life of a fly fisher, where you learn to wade slowly and softly, upstream if possible, and keep your casts short and your leaders long, light and supple so you work every pocket, each seam, as if they hold the 50-cm trout of your dreams—and often they do.

For a fly fisher, summer's ending is a noble time for thoughts of days past and of the future, of family, friends, life and your good fortune. It's a time of contemplation that no other season can offer. I relish it.

Caddis Flies

Grannom Caddis

Grannoms, nicknamed "black caddis" because they are almost black in some streams, is one of the key sedge hatches early in the spring and again late in summer and fall. They appear in swarms during late-August afternoons and evenings on rivers like the Stellako, Crooked and Blackwater in northern BC and a few weeks later on southern rivers.

Their emergence depends on falling water temperatures as rivers cool down after a period of warm summer days, and if conditions are right, thousands will fill the air in unison. During afternoon flights, many pupae will be emerging and hatching, a prime time to work with the Grannom DH Emerger (see p. 107); during evenings after mating, they will often return to lay their eggs by diving and swimming underwater to disperse their progeny. I hate using wet flies when trout are surfacing, but a Soft Hackle Emerger (see p. 94) swung through and under the surface film will often produce better results than a floating pattern when Grannoms are in an egg-laying stage.

October Caddis

This family of good-sized caddis flies, also known as Giant Orange Caddis on many northern American rivers, is one of the last major large insect hatches to be found in any freestone river system. They begin to appear in late August, and will continue to emerge sporadically through late October in most BC streams.

Because of this late-season activity, their hatching coincides with steelhead migrations of northwest BC rivers, thus you'll find many imitations of October Caddis used on skating and waking dry-fly patterns to persuade these giant rainbows to the surface. Some steelhead anglers are so desperate to win their prizes on the surface they will spend their entire several weeks of vacation time and thousands of casts to coax one fish to their dry fly—that's commitment!

October Caddis flies enjoy streams with moderate to fast flow, boulder and rocky bottoms, and ones with ample shoreline trees and vegetation. You won't find many in willow-lined, silty or slow-moving rivers like the Crooked in northern BC, but you will witness wonderful hatches in waterways such as the Stellako, Blackwater and McLeod, and bountiful displays in all of the Kootenay and southern Alberta west slope rivers.

Their larvae build cases by emitting a glue-like substance and pasting small pebbles, weeds and sticks to their exteriors, their coverings often looking like a decorator's den with vivid displays of coloured stones and grasses found on the stream's bottom. You'd almost think they were in competition for "best in show" by some of the spectacles they produce. Cased larvae, when nearing maturity, migrate to shallow shoreline rocks, get a toehold on their substrate and cling for dear life. There they will pupate and complete their metamorphisms until it's time to pop to the surface and hatch into the adult insect. When you see lots of cased caddis on the rocks you are clambering over take care to not disturb them, as these could soon be the fluttering insects you will catch your next trophy with.

Larva and pupa imitations are very good producers during months of August through October, fished floating lines with fine 5 to 6 X leaders, along shorelines, rolled along the bottom in less than 1 m of water. Both of these patterns are detailed in my first book, *Fly Fishing BC's Interior*.

Many patterns will duplicate the adult October Caddis: orange stimulators and humpies, small Salmonflies, Stimulators, Madam-X's or really, anything that is orange and floats. I've settled on the October Mikulak (see p. 107) for my happiness.

Hoppers

As you bustle along meadow-lined edges of streams during a late-summer afternoon, slashing through tall, dry grasses and disturbing foliage with your boots, hoppers scurry and flee from the commotion, and it's a good time to incorporate "hoppers" into your angling pleasure.

The life cycle of grasshoppers is interesting, going through stages of eggs, nymphs and five or six moults before becoming mature adults. Fertilized eggs are laid in pods by a female during late summer, buried in soil under grasses, the eggs hatching into immature nymphs late the following spring. Nymphs spend their summer going through moulting stages, each time shedding their skins before reaching maturity. Grasshoppers live only a year, adults dying off during first frosts before winter.

You will not often find trout sitting in shallow water waiting for a hopper "hatch," because they don't get to dine on as many hoppers as we think they do. As author Jeff Morgan wrote in a *Westfly* column: "Deep water, wind, and grassy banks are the trinity of good hopper fishing."

One way to create hopper activity to a knowing trout lie is to have a buddy walk the bank upstream of the run, chasing and scattering grasshoppers into the stream, some of which will float into the pocket you are fishing—barely bordering on proper fishing etiquette, but not illegal. Just a thought... but to remain friends you should take turns at this.

Hopper imitations are useful on rivers like the Bow and Elk for drift fishing out of a boat, but you must put them on the banks! Even a foot off the bank is not close enough. A useful tactic for stubborn browns and rainbows on the Bow River in southern Alberta is to drag your pattern off a likely-looking bank into a holding lie—if you're lucky enough to come away clean, you'll often hook up with a trophy trout.

Another effective hopper-fishing tactic is to *not* let them drift—keep them twitching, imitate their frantic struggles to get back to shore before they become trout food. If you can, fish them from the bank, well back to avoid detection by the fish, but close enough to control your casts, often placing only your tippet onto the water. Because a hopper-in-trouble's first instinct is to get back to the bank, its initial leg drive is shoreward, imitated by a few quick strips of your line; and, if you're lucky, the chase of a willing trout to your offering.

Some Stellako Hopper Revenge

I recall a glorious, magnificently coloured early-September day in 2009 on the Stellako River, fishing with friend (and personal editor) Bob Graham, just preceding the migration run of Fraser River sockeyes to Francois Lake and its tributaries. Big mature rainbows were holding in their usual prime runs, immature trout in the leftover water, all eagerly awaiting the arrival of their annual protein-laden larder of salmon eggs and spent carcasses that will fatten and nurture them through another long northern winter.

It was a delightful time of year—quiet, void of other fly fishers, about as lonely and pleasant as a trout river can get. The catching day began quickly in the bridge run, where the lengthening sun was already warming the river, producing sporadic popping of a few solitary caddis flies. Four nice trout came willingly to the Spotted Caddis (see p. 101) in the first run, and we keenly anticipated the outcomes of the river downstream.

A Trout to Remember

In a quiet glide he slumbers, a very large male rainbow of 58 cm hunkered into an undercut ledge that shelters him from predators: eagles, ospreys, minks and martens. He seldom rises to eat, preferring the wealth of larvae and nymphs drifting by him and the cover of darkness for his surface sojourns to intercept adult stoneflies, caddis flies and drakes. He is seldom fished for, as his lair is tricky to find, not by his intelligence, but by instinct for a safe place to live—and only a foolish fly fisher would hike the rough trail after darkness falls. And so he lives, waiting patiently for sockeyes to come in the fall, when he can once more fill his belly with the fat of roe and salmon skins that will sustain him until spring. He is king of his world!

But wait! In subdued light, a huge hopper splats onto soft water above him. It looks inviting, an easy, juicy meal—he rises from the bottom, within inches, and does not open his mouth but backs away. He is suspicious of the insect's movements. Perhaps some other time, he muses as he drifts back under his ledge. The fly fisher, excited by the fish's display, is discouraged but realizes the trout has not seen him, and may come again. He rests the glide, and watches. The trout is hungry, every few minutes showing by turning sideways and feeding in rhythms on drifting larvae and nymphs.

Hark! Too good to be true—again it comes, another hopper, closer to him. Overjoyed, he runs to grab it—too late, he's hooked. He fights well, up and down the river in strong aerial bursts, robust, deep runs of 50 m, until he is exhausted and succumbs to the relentless pressure. He rolls to his side, expecting death, and feels a firm but soft touch of hand, and freedom once more.

You can easily spend the entire day fishing the bridge runs in the Stellako because there are so many pockets, riffles and chutes to cover that it becomes imperative to fish all of the water. The wide inlet from the lake narrows after its first turn at the cabin pool; downstream from there you can fish the entire width of the Stellako on foot by wading its south bank.

I like to migrate about twenty to thirty minutes' hiking time downstream from the bridge in late mornings after the sun has had time to rise above the narrow, forested canyon on the south side and warm the water, which brings on expected surface insect activity. So downriver we went, happily clambering along the rough access trail that has only about twenty feet of level ground in its entire journey.

Spotted Caddis worked well, but only for small 30–40-cm trout—it was the larger ones we pursued, and they were reluctant to rise. I suppose we could have nymph-fished them, but for us, that's desperation tactics only.

Enter the hopper! Even though we were fishing canyon water, which is not hopper wealthy, the large trout we sought wanted size and quantity in their diet, and although a size #10 October Caddis (see p. 107) would probably also fit the bill, a size #8 Hopper (see p. 108) saved the day.

September: Time of Renewal

For some people, September is a time of death. They see it as waste and destruction, decay and loss of life. It's a time when summer birds have disappeared from our feeders, when forests are dank with the smell of rotting vegetation, when warm summer days lapse into frosty nights, and when, by the end of the month, the last forlorn kisses of autumn splendour begin to fade into winter's solemn grip.

But it's also a time of life and renewal. It's only fall, part of a natural cycle for all living creatures that depend on nature for their survival. As migratory birds fly south for winter, they take their young with them. Having survived their first year amidst the harshness of predators, and grown strong on rich summer feed, they will return next year to breed and renew the cycles of their ancestors. The greenery of deciduous trees turns brilliant with colour as the summer leaves whither and die, but their strong stalks will return next year when the warm winds of spring caress their buds and branches.

For many fish, fall is a time of ritual. For mature salmon, laden with fat and vibrant from ocean feeding on opulent planktons and crustaceans, summer has made them strong so that now they can face the final test of their existence—a race to the finish, one that will extinguish every last ounce of energy and reserves they have stored—and, after mating, their death. But in the passing of salmon, others may survive: trout that eat the salmon eggs and decaying skins; eagles and gulls that pluck out their eyes and tear at their skins; bears, wolves, minks and martens that gorge on their flesh; and finally, humans who pursue, catch and net them to feed their families.

In early spring, last fall's salmon death has been forgotten—not a trace remains, their remnants consumed by time, river and creatures. From the gravel of tiny streams and small rivers where their predecessors spawned and died, life is renewed. The low flows of winter and life-sustaining oxygen bubbling through the pebbles has spawned new salmon, fry that will once again flush to the oceans with the coming of spring freshets. As did their ancestors, some will grow and return to spawn several years later, while others will not.

As well as salmon moving homeward there are also steelhead, ocean-dwelling summer-run rainbow trout that travel the marine passages with the salmon, returning to their native streams where they will hold and overwinter in their chosen pools, spawn in spring and drift back to the ocean with the freshets. They too need the fall season to renew their species.

For mature lake, eastern brook and brown trout, fall is also their spawning time, after the abundance of summer feed has rendered them fat and healthy with reserves to breed and continue to live; for they, unlike the salmon, do not die after spawning, but live for many annual cycles of breeding. If their home river or lake supports salmon runs, they will flourish and be enriched from the salmon's death march; if not, they will grow strong on their environment's lush resources.

September is usually a month in which, for a short week or perhaps two, Indian summer can steal your heart away: chilly frosty mornings; warm shirtsleeve afternoons; golden yellow vistas, with cottonwoods, trembling aspens and poplars stealing the show; brilliant reds and purples cover the underbrush; and as for wind, breathless autumn days and nights.

The mean temperatures of September in northern BC are comparable to the month of May: average highs of 16°C, lows of 3°C. Early in the month, you'll often see highs of 20°C, but sure as your life, by the end of the month the honeymoon is over and you can bet on adding another layer of insulation to your body.

I welcome the seasons. Each has its own character and with it, challenges to overcome. Each fall, the gathering of winter wood can chew up several days, cutting into fishing time, but because of the hard physical work, winter seems more inviting with a warm, wood-heated home, and energy bills are more affordable. I enjoy watching wildlife gear up for the coming winter, especially the ones that stay for the duration: birds, as they gather their flocks and families together; squirrels, as they make busy rummaging and drying mushrooms, and storing seeds and nuts; and bears, foraging as they ready for hibernation, their coats shiny and bodies fat from late summer gorging.

Fishing Places

It is fall fishing that interests a fly fisher the most. Where I live in Central BC, many outdoors people hunt as well as fish, and the lure of the kill and fresh meat for the freezer takes them away from fishing our lakes and streams and into the backcountry with weapons and ATVs. Like fly fishers, they also get their fall fix, but by roaming the trails tracking our big game animals—moose, deer and elk. I've never been a hunter, but the exercise and its season appeals to me. I think if I should need to hunt, bow and arrow would be my choice of weapon.

Although summer's heat can linger through the first few weeks of September, rewarding a fly fisher with days that seem to be meant for fishing time, as in early spring it is once again a period in which lakes alter their chemistry and adjust their thermoclines. Summers in the north can often be warm (surely they are in the Cariboo and Southern Interior) and, without wind to stir the waters, extended hot spells late in August may result in an algae bloom that will loiter for a week or two, totally disrupting the attitude of fish by depleting their oxygen sources. Until the water temperature of the lake cools enough to stifle the algae, fly fishers feel as if they are casting into a bowl of pea soup. Even though lakes are fishable at this time by using sinking lines and presenting your flies below the bloom, fishing suffers, and when this happens on my favourite still waters I spend my time in rivers.

By late September, however, a lake's oxygen content is similar to spring conditions, well mixed throughout the system and dispersed with "happy" fish once again. An ideal September will drop the water temperature of lakes from 15°C in August to 10°C by month's end, triggering the beginning of a welcome feeding frenzy for fish. It's a good time to revisit my favourites.

In September, rivers of the Interior mountain valleys and plateaus are at perfect flows for fly fishing. They are small, as they were in August, and cooler but not frigid enough to be uncomfortable as in October and November when fishers need extra insulation under their waders. During the first few weeks of the month, river trout will still be looking up for their meals, challenging the last of the caddis hatches, and with the coming of the first few snotty, miserable days later in the month, will begin to seek Blue-Winged Olives for their surface enjoyment.

West slope cutthroat rivers of the Kootenays and southern Alberta, and the Bow River of Calgary offer perfect fishing in September, when hot late-summer days in the low country and frosty nights in the high country are common. I enjoy fishing these areas the week after Labour Day, when summer crowds have diminished, noisy dirt bikes are fewer, the campgrounds are only half full of visitors, and dry-fly fishing, until the first few snowfalls, is still the ticket for trout.

Steelhead rivers of the Skeena system that support summer runs— Morice, Bulkley, Babine, Kispiox, Copper and others of the watershed, and all of their tributaries—present their fabulous fisheries to worldwide visitors, many who have made the pilgrimage their vacation ritual for decades. They arrive in spite of seasonal storms on the North Coast that drift inland overnight and might blow out a river for days, and sometimes for the rest of the season. But they arrive in our land committed, faithful in their love for steelheads, and for the rivers where the fish swim.

Steelhead on the Morice and Bulkley Rivers

My friends and I don't necessarily go to steelhead rivers for the "catching." We go for the fishing, the sometimes one thousand fruitless casts, our love for the rivers the steelheads travel, and mostly, for the companionship of people who have the same empathy and understanding for the "noble"

Steelhead Trout—Survivors

I believe that steelhead trout are the most noble of all fish species. For fly fishers who seek them in BC waters, they are the ultimate challenge to bring to the fly. They are also the most affected species of anadromous (ocean going/river breeding) fish that man and his industries have unwittingly attempted to vanquish.

After adults spawn in early spring, well before their natal streams' freshets, fertilized steelhead eggs incubate and their fry emerge. They will remain and mature in their home freshwater streams for one to four years. Their instincts take over and when nature calls they migrate to the sea where they will spend one to five years in the marine environment before returning to their natal rivers. Less than 5 percent of the steelhead hen's eggs will survive to make the return journey. It's a phenomenon of nature that this staggered migration existence of their young in fresh and salt water shields the steelhead from extinction. Some rivers like the Kispiox in northwest BC and a few in Alaska produce fish in the 15–20-kg class.

A steelhead requires what seems to be very little to survive: clean mountain watersheds free from siltation, permitting oxygen-rich gravel filtration for their eggs' incubation; ample streamside forests and vegetation, to keep the streams cool for development of young fry; and adequate boulder, pool and canyon water, to provide resting areas and cover for their migrations and growth. It's an act of nature that our steelhead watersheds began this way when glaciers receded, and an insult to the fish that their habitat is in constant turmoil because of what we have allowed to happen to it.

Today, except for very remote migration streams along the North Coast of BC and Alaska, steelhead (and all anadromous species) that travel densely populated areas of the Pacific Ocean watershed must compete with human-generated obstacles that threaten their very existence. Two hundred years ago they were so prolific along the Pacific Coast that they were found as far south as northwestern Mexico. Today, however, you will rarely find them south of northern California.

Dale Freschi searching for steelhead at sunrise. Bulkley River below Smithers. Brian Smith photo.

Along the Pacific coastline, around populous coastal cities, we develop upstream dams and powerhouses on what were once major steelhead rivers, curbing the natural flows of their streams and raising water temperatures to unlivable limits for adult migrations and young fish fry. We pollute marine waters with human waste, fertilizers, pesticides, man-made disasters and even fish farms where the fish grow and mature. In their upper watersheds, we often log to shoreline their natal creeks and streams, silting them with unnatural runoff, unsuspectingly killing their unborn alevins. And on the high seas, we kill and market them as incidental casualties of drift nets. For decades, we allowed their estuaries to be net fished during their prime migration periods, limiting their natural numbers to those that could survive the carnage.

And still, the steelheads come back to us in summer running with the salmon, in winter on their own volition. Because of this incredible will to survive, they should be referred to as the "noble" species of fish.

Dale Freschi with a Morice River steelhead. Brian Smith photo.

trout. We also go to witness majesties of the autumn's season: the wind and scattering leaves in dry poplars and aspens; frosty, foggy mornings on the river; snowcapped mountain peaks and valley vistas on the horizons; and always, for the zip-zips of our fly lines as they cut the air and ply the lairs of steelhead runs.

The Morice River is a medium-sized stream, beginning as the outflow from Morice Lake high in the Morice Range, which flows in a northeast direction about 70 km toward the town of Houston, BC, where it meets "The Little Bulkley" River to form the larger Bulkley River. The Bulkley meets the Skeena River near New Hazelton, and is one of the Skeena's major fish-migrating streams, supporting about 30 percent of the Skeena fishery's run of steelhead, as well as sockeye, coho and chinook salmon species.

The Morice River is accessed from the Morice River Forest Service Road a few kilometres west of the town of Houston 305 km west of Prince George, the road cutting south from Hwy 16 West and following the river in a south-west direction about 70 km to its outlet at Morice Lake. For the self-contained camper, there are many roughly developed Recreation Site campsite locations along the river: Bymac (user pay) at the Telkwa FSR intersection at about the 4-km mark; Aspen Rec Site at 17 km; Owen Flats "A" RS at 28 km; Owen Flats "B" RS at 32 km; and Lamprey Creek RS at 43 km.

The Bulkley River begins as a small creek as it exits Bulkley Lake south of the little settlement of Rose Lake, which is the dividing line between the watersheds of the Fraser River system, which flow east from this summit, and the Skeena River system flowing west. The Bulkley gathers many creeks along its path to the Morice River confluence at Houston. West of Houston along its 130-km run to the Skeena at New Hazelton, it becomes a much larger system as it's met by two major tributaries, the Telkwa and Suskwa rivers.

There are no developed Forest Service Rec camping sites along the Bulkley. Perhaps this is because much of the river flows through private farm and ranching land. There are, however, several private RV parks along the route from Houston to Smithers that cater to the steelhead camping crowd. During steelhead season, when days are short and nights are chilly, I've found that motel units are happy, warm places to share with a buddy after a cold day on the rivers.

If you like to float and fish from drift, jet or pontoon boats, both the Morice and Bulkley are safe rivers to traverse. You must, however, avoid the unpassable canyon sections of the Bulkley below Smithers. All of the floats on the Morice can be worked from put-ins and take-outs at the recreation sites. On the Bulkley main stem, there are put-in accesses at Walcott, Quick, Telkwa and Smithers. There are others that require permission from landowners and registered guides—if you hire a guide for a few days, they know local places and hot spots for your fly-fishing pleasures. I've found the best sources for information on local conditions and guided fishing trips in the Bulkley Valley area are the knowledgeable people at Oscar's Source for Sports and McBike and Sport, both in Smithers.

Special regulations on the Skeena River main stem as well the Morice and Bulkley rivers have helped to maintain the world-class reputation of the salmonid runs they support: Classified Water, bait ban, single barbless hook and special closures. Please consult current regulations before planning your trip.

For the fly fisher, steelhead water is soft and stream flows can be worked methodically and thoroughly with a fly at river speed through thigh-deep runs. As fish work their way upstream from the ocean, in many cases a 300-km journey, they need to stop and rest. They will typically move through fast water, but rest at the top of these runs if suitable relaxation areas exist, often stopping for several days. Resting steelhead prefer soft water of walking speed, medium-sized boulders, depths of 1–2 m, inside current breaks and areas of inflowing highly oxygenated water from tributary creeks and streams; so should the fly fisher. These are prime areas to find steelhead resting, alert and willing to aggressively attack all intruders, including flies. The Morice and Bulkley rivers have this kind of fishing water on almost every corner and bend of the streams.

What flies to use, and what are the best times? The "old" steelhead logic of "Bright day, bright fly; dark day, dark fly" is quite true. It's also true that most steelhead are caught on sombre, dark days; that first and last light of fishing days are the best times; and that days of fog, cold air and crappy weather are good things. But I think the best time and place to go steelhead fishing is whenever you can in typical water. Keep your fly in the water from daybreak to darkness, and you should count hundreds of casts by the end of a few days, whether you have caught fish or not.

I love to tie steelhead flies, especially elegant styles from traditional patterns that used floss, tinsel, golden pheasant and mallard feathers and were trimmed with Spey hackles. Gosh, they're pretty! I continue to fish with these eye-catching, glamorous flies but am migrating toward some recent patterns that really catch steelhead when they are on the take. If I had to choose, I think a fly fisher can get away with three patterns for *all* of their steelhead fishing: an Intruder, leech-style fly tied in a combination of black, purple and electric blue; an egg pattern, tied in bubble gum pink; and a high-floating dry fly, perhaps a Mikulak-style caddis in neutral tone that can be turned into a waking fly.

One of my fishing partners, Dale Freschi, catches more steelhead in less time on the water than anyone I know. Ninety percent of his fish are caught on a trailing hook, stinger-style Intruder Leech using a Teeny T-200 fly line. I swear Dale can smell steelhead in a run. I believe if he lived close to a steelhead river like the Bulkley, he would catch hundreds of them in a season.

The first steelhead for Julian Franz and his proud daddy, Erich. Bulkley River. Neil Hodgson photo.

A Few Fish to Remember

The third week of September is a spectacular time to visit the Bulkley Valley with fly rod in hand. The rivers are in prime condition, and by this time enough steelhead have made the journey through the Skeena system to spread them over most runs and lies in both the Morice and Bulkley rivers.

It's also a good period to expect a fish to rise to the dry fly. Water temperatures are usually between 12 and 15°C at this time of year, plenty warm enough to attract late-season hatches of caddis flies, midges and mayflies. Although eating for sustenance isn't necessary for migrating steelhead because they are living off stored fat reserves, their freshwater existence several years past as young fry feeding on insects has stirred memories—they will instinctively attack surface flies if conditions are right and if they are in the mood.

Low light conditions—first light, last light, and cloud cover—will factor into the use of floating line, dry-fly techniques for steelhead.

Dale Freschi with a steelhead on Bulkley River. Brian Smith photo.

These settings are what they prefer, but in my experience bugs on the water will stir them as well. I caught my first dry-fly steelhead on a Brown Deer Hair Bomber size #12 a number of years ago on the upper Morice. It was on a warm, windless spectacular late October afternoon during a hatch of small caddis flies. I mused frantically as the silver 3-kg hen rose rhythmically for over an hour feeding on emerging Grannoms, stalking and willing her from every direction possible, before she finally took the fly as the day neared darkness. I'll never forget the little hen.

The runs through the Skeena were late in 2011, so we knew most of the fish would be in the middle of the Bulkley system, likely around Smithers to Houston. We stayed in a motel in Smithers and used partner Dale Freschi's new Hyde Power Drifter for our river runs, concentrating on the areas around town. The advent of power drifters is another addition to a steelheader's armoury of toys. It's essentially a flat-bottomed drift boat with a jet motor. You don't, however, require shuttle service or two vehicles as you do to operate an expedition with a pure drift boat; you can use one vehicle, put in at common launch ramps, motor upstream or downstream to your favourite fishing runs, and work your way back upstream, or drift or motor downstream to the next runs. They save a lot of time, extra vehicle expense and, when working downstream, often get you into prime fishing runs before the coming entourage of drifters work their way down to you. I'm not necessarily a competitive person who relishes this kind of one-upmanship stuff, but it isn't bad when you can get it.

The put-in at the Hwy 16 bridge before Smithers Park works well for the power drifter. Travelling west, you can access the park by taking the first right before the bridge, and the first left off this road to the all-vehicle launch site where there is room to safely park your trailer for the day. Over a span of three days we ran the boat upriver twice and downriver twice from Smithers, had time to try the Skeena south of Terrace, and also to fish the Bulkley upriver from the canyon off the Suskwa Forest Service Road on the way back from the Skeena. We didn't feel rushed or fished out and always made it back for supper hours, which is the kind of speed and versatility a power drifter or jet boat can add to your precious fishing days.

As I said, any steelhead trip is a crap-shoot. Did I mention Dale outfishes me ten to one when it comes to steelhead? We caught ten, and I caught one. Quite happily, I might add, because I have had trips where I fished three days without a pull. On the other hand, I've had trips of three days where I've caught ten, so who knows?

As we finished up on the third day, we watched the news over dinner hour, and saw the weather forecast that was to bring doom to the steelhead season on the Bulkley system. It rained steadily for the next three days, blowing the entire Skeena River system for the next three weeks. Dale and I caught it lucky. There were many tourists from all over the globe in the area who were not so fortunate, as they sat in motel rooms, campers and resorts with fly rods strung, watching their precious annual holidays wash down the river. And that, my friends, is steelhead fishing at its best, and worst.

Bow River, Calgary, Alberta

Touted as one of the finest "city" trout streams in the world, the Bow River has earned this reputation by offering anglers arguably the largest number of average trophy-sized (over 50-cm) rainbow and brown trout you can expect to tangle with on any trout stream on the planet.

How did this occur? The answer lies in the river's beginnings, in its endings, and generally in its makeup—some man-made, but much of it natural. For a trout river like the Bow to produce an abundance of trophy-class fish, it requires several components: pristine headwaters; regulated flows; abundant and prosperous insect populations for growth; and mostly, ample tributaries for adult spawning resources and safe rearing habitats for young fry. Much of its glory can be attributed to the influence of dams on the Bow above Calgary.

The Bow River begins as ice-melt of the Bow Glacier, part of the Wapta Icefield lying in the Rocky Mountains, which forms Bow Lake, situated beside Hwy 93 on the Banff-to-Jasper route. From Bow Lake, the river flows south to Lake Louise, and then turns eastward to course through Banff, Canmore, Cochrane and Calgary. At Calgary, the Bow turns south-east, its splendid valley meandering through rich prairie ranchlands, finally meeting with the Oldman River on the grassy plains west of Medicine Hat. It's a long journey of almost 600 km from its source high in the Rockies, not without challenges if it wants to become a "blue ribbon" trout stream.

The Bow River's best fly-fishing water can be divided into four sections: the upper Bow above Banff; the upper Bow between Banff and the first dam at the town of Seebee; the Bow between Calgary and the Carseland weir; and finally, the Bow below Carseland.

The first section of the upper river above Banff contains the prettiest water on the river, where mountains meet stream, and below Banff, where stream meets rolling foothills and prairie. It's gorgeous country, the water clean and cold, but it lacks the nutrients and warmth to grow trophy trout. There are, however, populations of bull trout that relish this kind of water and smidgeons of smaller rainbows, cutthroats and brown trout scattered throughout the system. It's spectacular scenery, but I'm thinking it shouldn't be a fly-fishing destination when the best water is but an hour east!

Between Banff and Seebee, a 30-km stretch of the Bow, fly fishing improves greatly, but it's the brown trout that will tickle your fancy. The Bow in this section and farther on its route to Calgary is influenced by key factors such as the addition of several tributaries—the Kananaskis River from the south, the Ghost River from the north, and Jumping Pound Creek, also from the south—and the nutrients of treated phosphates and nitrates entering the river from wastewater plants at the towns of Banff and Canmore.

The Calgary-to-Carseland section of the Bow is where the river gets its reputation as a world-class fishery. As Calgary author Jim McLennan writes in his fine book *Trout Streams of Alberta*, the Bow is "probably Canada's most famous trout stream." It's a fabulous piece of trout water, propagating both rainbows and browns, its flow moderately regulated by two dams above Calgary and properly fertilized by the treatment plant that gathers several million flushes of toilet water daily from the fastest-growing city in Canada. This sounds like an act of treason to a trout stream, but appropriately built, handled, treated and regulated, the dams on the Bow River for about 100 km below Calgary are proof that dams and sewerage can actually make an otherwise nutrient-poor river into one of the finest portions of trout water in the country.

To make it work, the prairie flatland gives the Bow its shallow and moderate gradient, dams provide reservoirs for drinking water and regulate the flow, treated sewage and runoff from city streets offer chemical nutrients that foster abundant weeds and plants, insects thrive on the enriched plant life, and trout get big and feisty, growing shoulders from their insect smorgasbord. Add to this mixture the Highwood River and its tributaries entering this section of the Bow about halfway to Carseland, which are the spawning habitats for mature trout and a nursery for young fry, and you have the perfect marriage between people, river and trout.

Below the Carseland weir, although the fishing remains similar to the *best* section above the weir, public access is limited to permission granted through the Blackfoot Indian Reserve band office at Gleichen. Getting a permit can be hit and miss, but it's worthwhile if you wish to fish in less crowded water. Once you meet the Bassano Dam at the end of the reserve water, the Bow becomes ordinary. With nutrients finally flushed from its

Kevin Smith with a gorgeous rainbow trout. Highwood River, Alberta.
Brian Smith photo.

system, the Bow remains an average, though sometimes surprising, trout stream along its confluence to the Oldman.

Calgary to Carseland

If you're a tourist visiting the Bow for your first time, or a casual returnee, this is the section you'll want to concentrate your efforts on. It's prime trout water, holding good populations per kilometre of oversized browns and rainbows, and is easily navigable "Class 1" water from the city to the weir at Carseland.

Although you can walk and wade from many access spots on the middle Bow, it's a busy, competitive river. Your best chances to connect with fish are to float the river by pontoon or drift boat, or to hire a guide for a day or two through the Calgary fly shops. These shops are critical to your success if you don't know the river. They offer access maps to walking trails, details of roads that access the put-ins and take-outs, shuttle services, pontoon and drift boat rentals, local fly patterns that work and, mostly, local knowledge of hatches in progress. All of this will take you several days to work out if you are trying to figure out the river on your own.

The Bow is a gentle stream below Calgary. The biggest issue to fishing success is your ability to read the abundant soft water, recognize the structures that trout will lie in or against, and your skill at handling a boat to get good drifts and not disturb the runs you'll want to get out to fish. As with most heavily fished trout rivers, the Bow performs best on miserable rainy days that make you think twice about going fishing, or during the subdued light of dawn or twilight. Many fly-fishing Calgarians who know the river intimately will only fish when the sun is off it, or during the week when fishing pressure subsides. Its moodiness reminds me of my favourite home stream in northern BC—the Stellako. These two rivers take time to know and understand, and dues should be paid by embracing their grumpy days as well as their banner days. Rewards are gained by learning and loving them unconditionally.

What are some good fly patterns for the Bow? For the big browns and rainbows when there is no hatch activity going on, most fly fishers pound the banks and seams with streamers, woolly buggers, Hare's Ear Nymphs, stoneflies and, ugly but true, San Juan Worm patterns. During hatch periods, dry flies rule—small ones, sizes 14 through 20, with standard patterns like Elk Hair Caddis, Pale Morning Duns, Tricos and Blue-Winged Olives (see p. 94). Dry flies for fishing while drifting are the usual suspects: stonefly imitations like the Salmon Fly (see p. 103) and Golden Stones (see p. 104), and hopper patterns (see p. 108) during mid- and late summer. Many fly fishers on the drift believe in the stimulator or hopper with dropper method (legal in Alberta): a floating indicator, with a small nymph hanging 30 cm below the floater—most trout take the dropper.

There are three good day-long floats in the Calgary-to-Carseland section: Policeman's Flats to McKinnon Flats, McKinnon to Janzen's, and Janzen's to Carseland. I've done them several times with my sons, Kevin and Graham, and the jury is out as to which one is best. Kevin lives in Calgary, owns a nice drift boat, and floats the river ten to twenty days per season. I think he likes Policeman's to McKinnon best, but then again,

A Good Drift

I fondly remember the best day I have had on the Bow, drifting the river from Janzen's to Carseland with Kevin and Graham. I try not to keep count so I have to guess here, but I'm thinking a twenty-fish day is about right. It was a bright day in late September, a week that gave us a dump of snow a few days previously while fishing the Oldman River and its tributaries.

Basking in sunlight for most of the day, in typical Bow fashion the trout hung in the middle of the river and sucked nymphs, not even thinking about venturing onto the flats for the smorgasbord of insects that were hatching periodically—small pale caddis, water boatmen and a couple of species of mayflies, commonly known as pale morning duns and Blue-Winged Olives (BWOs). It was nice to see the BWOs begin to come—it usually takes a few days of snotty weather in September to get them moving.

We struggled to catch fish for most of the day, Kevin managing a few over-sized browns while pounding the banks on the drift with a white marabou streamer, Graham and me sucking it up trying to be good sports. After all, *we were fishing.*

As afternoon wore on, the day grew longer on the catching scale, but after a quick sandwich for dinner a few clouds rolled in, which softened the light. Prospects for an evening rise looked almost possible as hatches of caddis and BWOs became more intense. Trout began to move off the shelves and into the soft bank water and easy glides, chasing the fluttering pale caddis hatch that had intensified as the last few hours of daylight quietly ebbed from the sky.

We could see the Carseland weir, which is a few kilometres downstream from this section of river, but after a long day of not much catching, this was what we were waiting for—the Bow to come alive, as it invariably does if you wait long enough. We took fish after fish, lengths up to 50 cm, hard-running rainbows that had avoided the bright sun all day, only to become idiots as their inhibitions left them with the fading light. Fishing one small piece of bank water, I stood in one place and took nine trout on successive casts using a #14 Caddis Blonde, Mikulak style (see p. 97). These are the Bow River days you remember, knowing the fish are there, being lucky enough to wait them out and having the correct pattern when they do come on.

like a lot of fly fishers, he kind of keeps things to himself when he finds a fishing spot he likes.

My personal favourite is Janzen's to Carseland—I like the structure of braided seams, islands and broken riffles, and find the soft channel water just above Carseland quite intriguing.

Alberta—the Southern Rivers

When our family lived in Sherwood Park, Alberta, for a short eighteen months ten years ago I struggled to find good trout water, and reasoned why most northern Albertans prefer golf over fishing—there is a multitude of good golf courses, but very few viable places to wet a line for trout. Oh, you can fish walleyes to your heart's content, but try to find a trout stream or lake that isn't an irrigation ditch, weed-infested slough or former gravel pit! And the Rockies at Hinton or Rocky Mountain House weren't close enough (for me) to be called "home water." I enjoyed the people, but was secretly happy when northern BC came knocking on my door again. After all, I am a trout fisherman.

The west slope cutthroat and rainbow trout streams of southern Alberta are a different matter. The ones I have come to love begin as little trickle creeks, originating from snowmelt high on the Rockies' east slopes, find their home valleys, and instigate their daring rushes to their mother river, the Oldman, finally traversing quietly through the prairie grassland valleys and emptying into the South Saskatchewan River near Medicine Hat, Alberta.

The Oldman River's major tributaries—Willow Creek and the Crowsnest, Castle, Livingstone and Waterton rivers—are synonymous

Step falls on Castle River, Southern Alberta. Brian Smith photo.

with Alberta trout fishing. Each has its own myriad of tributary feeders; small creeks, most of them less than the width of a car lane, perfect spawning and nursery streams for the greater rivers; gorgeous brooks for walk-and-wade trout fishing, chock full of native trout to 45 cm. These little creeks are perfect places to teach your children the art of fly fishing, while showing them the beauty of natural mountain scenery and the benefits of good exercise as they explore each bend and pool of a little stream. Many can be fished on a tight budget, without waders, wearing ankle-high running shoes, shorts and with a minimum of equipment—the way we started many decades ago.

I commend the Alberta government for having the foresight in the 1990s to protect their rivers from overkilling. Their kill ban on bull trout saved the fragile trout from extinction and the bag-limit reductions on cutthroat has rejuvenated their populations in native streams. Rivers are not like lakes; they are not as fertile or easy to stock. Fish inventory can be wiped out by overfishing, allowing unhealthy kill limits and the use of barbed hooks and bait. Now if we could only keep ATVs and dirt bikes from crossing creeks and rivers and tearing out the gravel beds...

If you plan a trip to this area, pick up the *Backroad Mapbook Southern Alberta* by Mussio Ventures, available at local fly-fishing shops, and you mustn't pass through Bellevue on Hwy 3 without stopping at one of the best little fly shops in Alberta, Vic Bergman's Crowsnest Angler. Vic offers a complete selection of fly-tying supplies and equipment, a good assortment of productive local patterns, advice on the current hot spots plus guided services to the many creeks and rivers of this splendid area of the country. And while you're at it, pick up Jim McLennan's *Trout Streams of Alberta* from the shop as well—it covers the entire east slope of the Rockies drainage in great detail.

These creeks and rivers open to fishing the first week of July, after spring runoff, the exception being the Crowsnest River, which is open year-round for those discerning fly fishers who are willing to jump on the opportunity to brave winter winds, ice-laden banks and frigid water to nymph fish for oversized rainbows in their overwintering pools. For some Calgarians and a smidgeon of local anglers, a February chinook from west of the Rockies starts their hearts pumping; they can't resist the lure of the Crowsnest, and who can blame them for their follies?

Dry-fly patterns for this part of the country should be mostly on the small side of the spectrum: sizes 14–20 in Elk Hair Caddis (see p. 101), Blue-Winged Olives (see p. 94), Adams (see p. 95), Tricos (see p. 105), PMDs (see p. 105) and Ants (see p. 110). The exception for size again will be the Crowsnest, which has an incredible hatch of salmon flies (stoneflies) that peaks later in June, and where you will need to use Stimulators and Salmon Fly (see p. 103) patterns in sizes 4–6. During July, Golden Stones (see p. 104) in sizes 8–10 and Green Drakes (see p. 104) in sizes 12–14 will be the attractor table fare; hoppers are well received by trout during the dog days of August and early September.

Nymph patterns will always work on these streams, especially when there are no hatches prevalent. Reluctant as I am to use them, every now and then you need to just keep pace with your fishing buddy who is dragging the stream in front of you with a San Juan Worm or likely substitute—sometimes you have to choose your buddies more carefully!

You should come armed with the usual suspects: an assortment of small nymphs in sizes 12–18 such as Bead Head Pheasant Tails (see p. 93), Hare's Ear Nymphs (see p. 93), Prince Nymphs, Flashbacks (see p. 93) and Soft Hackle Emergers (see p. 94); a gathering of large nymphs like black and golden stoneflies in sizes 6–10; and even, I suppose, some San Juan Worms for the picky Crowsnest.

On the Crow

In late July 2011, I enjoyed another blissful week of dry-fly fishing the Kootenays and Alberta streams with Kevin, my eldest. We had kicked the hell out of the Elk system for a week, and wanted to take a crack at the Crowsnest. Neither of us knew the river well enough to say that we knew where to fish it and local knowledge is somewhat secretive—"There she is; you guys look like pros, go figure her out yourself." Some helpful advice from my buddy Dale Freschi, who grew up in the Koots and tries to catch the annual late June salmon fly hatch on the Crow, took us into a piece of water that is, in a word, *amazing*. So we found and traversed the unmarked dirt road, hid the vehicle and picked our way down the well-used trail and through the wader-ripping barbed wire fence, both time-worn by thousands of fly fishers before us—some secret, eh?

At first glimpse of the canyon run, I was speechless. The river is gradient, its steps pronounced but gradual, not challenging for wading but requiring a thoughtful crossing to get at the best-looking water. It turns a few corners in this section, making deeper depressions in the far banks, cutting bends and seams on inside curves as it pummels through the short canyon and around great boulders on its course downstream. Rocky outcrops and gravel bottom, large and small stones, deep pools, fast riffles— perfect stonefly water! Golden stones it is.

It didn't take long—first cast in the first run and I was into my best fish of the day. Crowsnest rainbows are chunky from their good diets, and I was thinking this trout was all my little 3-weight, 8-foot Powell could handle in this fast water. I've caught many larger fish on this rod (mostly cutts), but after several runs into the backing and downriver, working this 50-cm specimen back upriver was giving me a "go." The feisty trout finally succumbed and was released. Needless to say, I was pleased because this was my first trout on the "Crow."

We worked upstream from that first pool, criss-crossing the river into more pools and runs, and I caught two more on the same Golden Stone fly, identical sizes of the first at 50 cm, give or take. Some say this river is "tough fishing," and I agree; but then again, timing is everything when trout fishing. It was a good day, one I will affectionately remember in my dreams when the deep snows of a northern BC winter take me back to the Crow.

Fly Patterns for September

Still-water Lakes

Many days in September are without wind, the glory of lingering autumn colours overwhelming to the sensuous person. The calm days and soft light are reminders of summer's last gasps of true warmth, and for us northerners late summer days are delightful, but also a message that winter is around the corner.

By September, major hatches of insects have subsided on your favourite lakes. You'll come across minor midge and chironomid hatches during this time period, but they will be small in size. It's a good opportunity to fish the larva stage of the insect, reverting to bloodworm patterns slowly worked through the littoral zone at a snail's pace.

Freshwater shrimp are once again the main diet of trout. We have a few good scud lakes in our northern region of the province, usually the ones with extensive shoals like Hobson, Chief Grey, Tory, Vivian and Dragon. The Cariboo and Southern Interior still waters will be infested with the year's young immature. The sizes will be small, and it's often a size 16 or 18 Hyalella (see p. 86) that will make your day, fished in the shallows with a floating line—I guarantee trout will be looking for them; it takes a lot of shrimp to fill their bellies.

There will also be the odd caddis around. If trout are rising around the lakeshore, go after them with a Mikulak size 10 in a rusty orange colour, which imitates the big October Caddis (see p. 107), or a dun-coloured caddis size 12 to replicate random leftovers from traveller sedges that have been hatching through the summer months, and will continue to stir surface activity on the shoals from interested trout.

Leeches roam the shallows of lakes all the time and are often keyed upon when other hatches aren't present, but keep your patterns small in the fall, about size 12, which imitates the maturing young leeches that trout prefer. Fish them deeply and slowly with full-sinking lines, and floating line and fluorocarbon leader if you can see the bottom of the lake, which will allow you the benefit of a long, painfully slow retrieve through the proper lowest zone of the water table.

September is famous for its ant hatches. In all of my fifty-odd years of fishing lakes, I've managed to catch an ant hatch on only a few occasions. The first time I was in my early twenties, didn't have a pattern to match the swarm of red ants that were in flight everywhere on the lake, and could only wish and want for one. Of course, the next day I promptly found a pattern in a magazine and tied some, which sat in my fly box for twenty years before I needed them again. I'll share a good story later in this chapter.

The most prolific and reliable two-week hatch (or flight) in September is the activity that comes with the annual flying trip of water boatmen and backswimmers. Along with ants, it's the last excitement of the dry-fly season on our lakes.

Water Boatman and Backswimmer

For water boatmen and backswimmers, these late summer days and cool frosty nights are perfect settings for their nuptial flights. For fly fishers, it's a last chance for one of the biggest "hatches" of the fishing season, which is really not a hatch per se, but a flight.

Boatmen and backswimmers are rarely fish food during the summer, preferring to stay well hidden among weeds and bottom debris as they dine and scavenge their meals on the lakes' abundant resources of shrimp, mayflies, midge larvae and daphnia. They haunt the shallows of lakes and creeks and are air breathers, often observed popping to the surface to gather an air pocket, which is carried under their abdomens in the form of a bubble.

You'll differentiate water boatmen from backswimmers by size, colour and swimming action. The water boatman is 6–10 mm long by 3 mm wide with grey-brown markings on its hard, cased back and pale yellow to tan belly colourations. The backswimmer is larger, about 10–15 mm long by 5 mm wide with a dark brown back and brown-olive belly. Water boatmen swim belly-down; backswimmers belly-up. Both look silvery in appearance because they swim with their air bubbles for breathing trapped under their bellies. This characteristic is important to impart in any fly patterns you tie to imitate this insect, usually by the addition of silver Mylar, tinsel or clear plastic.

It's the mating call that arouses them in fall, taking advantage of windless days to take flights and copulate. If it's windy, they won't fly, because their flights will blow them into shore where they will die without water.

Water boatmen are more palatable to fish than backswimmers, perhaps because backswimmers can impart a vicious bite and are less digestible. I don't think fish are discerning enough to notice the difference when they are both in their flight stages because they are both hammered greedily during periods of mating activity. (See Water Boatman and Backswimmer, p. 109.)

Ants

A fly fisher had better have an ant pattern in the bag for the month of September. Whether you fish lake or stream, when they fly forth to colonize another ant hill, they are relished by trout. I think they would be quite bitter, but who am I to guess what a fish should or should not like to eat? Consider their appetites for worms and leeches.

Perhaps it's the colour red-orange, but I think red ants seem to be more desired by trout than black ones. I understand the larger carpenter ants also have flight periods, apparently in mid-summer, but I have never seen them fly near lakes that I fish. Fly fishing is an amazing pastime—unless you fish every day like some lucky fools who make it their living (yes, you, John Gierach, one of my favourite fishing writers), you may only witness a few major ant hatches in your lifetime.

If you run into an ant flight on a lake and have tied a good ant pattern, it's probably in your "river" box back in the truck, or at home because you are fishing lakes this day. This paradigm has happened to me often enough that I now carry an assortment of my river patterns just to cover those oddball days that I need one on a lake.

That "ant hatch" thing happened to me on September 26, 2010, while fishing Dragon Lake with Dale Freschi. My diary says we were having a tough day on the lake. At about 3 p.m., however, on a warm, windless afternoon, out of the cottonwoods flew red ants, many of them slapping the water, sticking in the surface film, struggling to regain flight. Very large trout patrolled the shoreline, picking off ants like lollipops. Fortunately, I did have my river boxes with me. Unfortunately, these were big trout, my floating line and 4-weight rod was strung with 2-kg test tippet, and I mused to my partner that my odds were fifty-fifty on landing what I could catch.

The big bugger took the first little #16 Red Ant (see Ants, p. 110) I threw at him, jumped a couple of times and then ran head-down into the weeds. We jostled back and forth for ten minutes, him in control, as my tackle was so light I had to keep it tight and let him charge around until either he won or I did. Finally, he turned to his side and let me net and release him—60 cm long, 4 kg, my best trout of the year.

The only time I like a stiff rod with lots of backbone is when I fish steelhead or salmon. All of my trout fishing is done with light, moderate-action rods that give me a feel for my fish and an easy swing when I cast them, more like jazz music than hard rock. I build my own fly rods, and am quite partial to twenty-year-old technology, like IM6 graphite, which imparts a bend from the tip to the grip. My favourites are: a 4-weight, 9-foot Sage LL (Light Line) for lakes; a 3-weight, 8-foot Powell Legacy Light for small creeks and rivers; and a 4-weight, 8½-foot IM6 Anglers Workshop house blank for larger rivers and lakes. They don't have the distance power for 90-foot casts, but they have the softness of feel and bend strength that won't break many tippets, they load effortlessly, and the only thing that shatters them is screen doors. Perhaps one day I'll try bamboo, as purists say they too are effortless, but every time I pick one up, it feels heavy to me.

Steelhead Flies

It's a moot point what attracts a steelhead to strike at your fly: curiosity, aggression, anger, territorial response, or just plain inherent instincts? Generally, it's not a feeding reply; they have genetically harboured enough reserves from their ocean-feeding frolics to last them the several months that they require to journey to their home streams, spawn and, in many cases, return to the ocean.

So, what we are looking for when we design and fish steelhead patterns are to key on the fish's response that will trigger its primal senses and entice the trout to strike at your fly. In designing sinking flies, look to achieve subtleness with dark colours such as black and purple, but add flash to spark interest and aggression in the fish's reply by incorporating Polar Flash, tinsel and fluorescent blue to the mix. All of these features are apparent in what I call the Steelhead Intruder (see p. 111), a style and colour of fly that has been a top producer in the northwest for the past decade or so.

It's a well-known fact that the colour pink turns steelhead on. Not only is pink the colour of washed-out roe, it's also the colour of rotting fish flesh. This is where the steelhead's instincts and territorial habits play their part—if it's edible and in my space, I'll get rid of it by eating it. It's the natural thing to do. So, we tie egg patterns (see p. 111) and slinky marabou-style flies in colours of pink and orange, which cater to this response.

Dry flies are a different matter. Why will a steelhead shoot through 2 m of water to viciously attack a floating fly? We can only reason it's the fish's response to their ancestry—when they were young trout fry, they would rise for bugs on the water, the bigger insect the better. Most of the dry flies that attract steelhead in the fall are caddis imitations: Mikulaks, Bombers, Stimulators and the like. The only big bug coming off the water in September–October is the October Caddis, so there you have it—a feeding response ingrained in their genetics as they were growing up.

Your choice of sinking fly line will also have a bearing on your steelhead success. You *must* get your fly to the fish, whether in 1 m of water or 3 m. I've tried them all, spent hundreds of dollars on fly lines and sinking tips of all types and purpose that are *supposed* to put me into fish. They have all worked at times. I think, however, judging by hook-up success, one of the best all-purpose lines for steelhead fishing in rivers is the Teeny 200. For comfort, it's light enough to cast nicely (unlike the Teeny 300 and heavier); for success, the line is heavy enough to sink into the fish-lying zone, as long as the depth of the river is less than 2 m.

October: Last Bites

For me, living in the Central Interior, October means fishing time is quickly petering out. By this time, I've typically clocked between forty and fifty days fishing *somewhere* since the ice left the lakes in April, and even though I'm never ready to give up on my fishing year, time is moving on without me.

In Central BC, October's climate is like April, in that it's difficult to predict what will happen with the weather. I've fished in shirtsleeves on 15°C days in mid-October, but there have been other years when Thanksgiving weekend has been my last outing on lakes. Sure as death and taxes, we will get a dump of snow in October, and if it stays, winter and snow is here until next April. October is the first month of fall that sinks below double-digit average highs, waddling through the period with an average daytime high of 9°C and evening low of -1°C.

The problems associated with late-fall fishing are usually the barometer and changing weather patterns. Storms, falling barometers, strong winds from the north and east—all of these spell doom for fishers trying to coax a few last days of the season from a lake. It's all too often that your best fishing will occur in a few short bursts during the day, but you have to put the whole day in to get that energy from the fish. A hard frost

Erich Franz with his best-ever steel-head at Morice River. Cal Tant photo.

will rarely result in poor fishing. I tend to draw the line at about 5°C—if the daily high reaches that mark, my guides will not ice up and I can dress warmly enough to conquer the cold. If combined with a 20-km/h hour wind, however, 5°C seems like -10°C, so I'm staying home.

Migratory songbirds have been gone for many weeks. Geese, sandhill cranes, ducks and loons have long vacated their northern nesting grounds of marshes, lakes and beaver ponds, and are hurriedly making their journeys south for the winter.

Fishing Places

October is "big fish" time in still-water lakes. As water temperatures of lakes hover between 5–10°C, oxygen is dispersed evenly throughout the water column, and you'll find trout scattered everywhere, especially on the shoals, where most of the aquatic insects have spent the summer and are still there in abundance because of their breeding cycles. As winter approaches, many insects will migrate to deeper water for overwintering. October is a very good time to concentrate your fly-fishing efforts in less than 4 m of water. I'll spend a lot of time searching high-quality lakes for their trophy rainbows: Dragon, Opatcho, Marmot, Hobson and many others.

Trout rivers begin to hibernate. The last flashes of fall splendour leave their banks desolate-looking and the water turns to a grey and unsettling cold, mysterious cast. The busy summer of insect hatches and migrations is but a persistent memory of what a trout river can be. It's fall, almost time for a rest, soon to be winter, when days are even shorter and nights longer, and when our rivers can have all the slumber they need.

Many of our best trout rivers, ones that entertain sockeye salmon runs like the Stellako and Horsefly rivers and many others in the Interior, could not sustain their angling qualities without the life-giving abundance of salmon eggs and carcasses. October is a trout's prime time for bulking on protein, as pods of sockeye salmon arrive daily through the weeks of late September to the end of October. The river's resident trout and coarse fish will follow the sockeyes upriver from pool to run, uninhibited, almost oblivious to predators, dangers and fishers. For the fly fisher, they are almost too easy to catch with egg patterns, the trout's only intent honed on gorging on sockeye eggs.

In the rivers of the northwest, the Skeena and Kitimat, their tributaries and others, October is perhaps the most reliable time for the fly fisher who searches for steelhead. Bolstered by salmon that have been filling and flushing through the tributary systems during late-summer months, the rivers' lies and pools are now holding their finest sport fish—summer steelheads. They quietly overwinter in their home streams, waiting and holding until the next spring, when they will hopefully spawn and return to the ocean with the coming freshet. Some won't have the reserves to survive and will die; others will persist. It is nature's way, however, that the genetically strong will endure to return to the ocean for strengthening and will once again make the arduous journey to their natal streams.

By late October, most of the salmon have spawned and died, their carcasses spread over thousands of kilometres of lakes, creeks, rivers and ocean estuaries. They have come in numbers, by the thousands and millions; none will return to the sea. They have given the last of their lives to the rivers and the creatures that inhabit them, asking nothing in return but the chance to reproduce and extend their species.

My friends and I will fish the lakes and rivers in October, often in chilly and damp weather conditions as the coming winter approaches, but eager with the anticipation that our largest trout of the year will present itself on the next cast. We will treasure the last days of the fishing year, and be thankful for another year of health and good fortune.

October on the Stellako

The Stellako River's sockeye salmon arrive in late September after an epic journey that has brought them from their feeding and maturing grounds in the Gulf of Georgia and beyond to the Fraser River mouth at Richmond, and onward to their birthplaces in the tributaries of Francois Lake and in the Stellako. Their migration paths have consumed well over a thousand kilometres of waterways and meandering river channels as they swim upriver to their natal water. To reach the Stellako, they begin at the Fraser's mouth in Georgia Strait (the Salish Sea), ascend the Fraser north to Prince George, turn west at the Nechako River, west at the Nautley River (shortest river in BC), swim through Fraser Lake and into the Stellako.

It's an impressive journey, the sockeye in full red plumage, ripe as mature tomatoes by the time they enter the river. Some will spawn in the Stellako; most will continue their path through Francois Lake and into the lake's tributaries. After hatching from stream gravel the following spring, the young sockeye live in Francois or Fraser Lake for one to three years before many migrate down the Fraser River system to the ocean. In four to six years the migrating sockeye will return to the Stellako to spawn and die, so ending the short but successful life of a sockeye salmon.

By Thanksgiving weekend, it's a quiet time for fly-fishing traffic on the Stellako. Summer visitors are long gone, insect hatches on the river are sparse, and only a few locals who know the river system and are not out hunting are willing to brave the sometimes inclement weather of mid-October. The sockeye run reaches its peak; rainbows and whitefish stack up in the pools and runs, bunting eggs from the ripe, weary female salmon when they can, and fleeing from the aggressive male that chases them from his selected breeding mates.

Very few trout will look up now; dry flies are fruitless. It's a time for drifting single-egg patterns into the runs and pools where the salmon are resting, gathering energy for the final push to their spawning grounds. Their urge is relentless, ever forward, guided by their sense of smell and the pull of the sun.

In a ritual that I have repeated many times over the last twenty years, I was joined this time by fishing partner, Dale Freschi, and "Big Al" Dunbar,

Shane Lake, one of Prince George's "city" lakes on a fall afternoon.
Richard Barrie photo.

a friend of mine and Dale's from Calgary. I've told my fishing buddies on many occasions that they must take time from their annual steelhead treks and give the Stellako a go in October.

When we arrived to launch our pontoon boats at the Glenannan Bridge for the run down the river, it was a frosty morning, clear and cold but breathtaking. The two-hundred-year-old cottonwoods that salute the bridge run were still in fall splendour, their leaves golden and glimmering in the early morning sunlight. The river was in perfect condition for our float, high enough to cover the boulders in the middle of the channel with ample clearance to navigate the edges of the runs, to keep from disturbing the trout stacked behind the sockeye. Thousands of sockeye were finning purposefully in the heads of the bridge runs, waiting their turn to push upriver into beckoning Francois Lake.

As Dale and Al prepared their crafts for launching, I took advantage of the opportunity to make a few casts at the bridge run, knowing where the trout would be piled, intimately aware of the lies and pockets in this section of the river after spending many days plying its riffles and runs during the summer season. My second drift of the egg fly (see p. 111) brings a hefty pull and a nice 1-kg rainbow to the rod, which dances and then takes a frantic run well into my backing as he escapes his pool, the current his ally now, testing the resistance of my Sage 4-weight fly rod. It's over for him after several strong runs, the darkly striped mature male rainbow turning to his side and released quickly to his river. It was a good start, with indications of what was to be a great day of fly fishing.

The river is gin-clear in October, and as we drifted over the schools of sockeye, trout and whitefish, they parted east and west, and then scurried in all directions, only to reform their groups quickly as the pontoon boats glided through their runs. The Stellako is low this time of year. You need to float the edges, if possible, and keep out of the main runs to keep fish from spooking, but the flow will often dictate your safest path, which is usually down the middle of the river. The fish, however, are so focused on their gorging that your presence is only a temporary nuisance to them, and they recover from their brief startle in a hurry. We find that after slicing through a run it's best to rest a pool for a few minutes and let it settle before beginning to fish, because it seems the best fish take the longest to resume their positions after a scare.

The top 7 km of river above the falls contains 80 percent of the Stellako's trout inventory, and the best fishing water. You should focus on these sections, especially the soft segment of pocket water about 2 km below the bridge, where sight fishing for stacked-up rainbows will make your heart pound as they dash to intercept your fly in water so crystal clear you can watch them attack it as the fly floats along its drift.

The falls below the power lines at 7 km require a short, easy portage—*stay river left* as you pass under the power lines. Below the falls there are only a few sweet spots that hold trout, found on the inside and outside corners of a few runs where the Stellako turns as it meanders out of the hills, canyons and dense evergreen forest into a flat meadow lined with willows, poplars and cottonwoods.

Be warned. Even though the water below the falls looks boring and shallow, this is the area of the river that is most dangerous, as poplars and cottonwoods can often be found uprooted and lying across the narrow river. On two occasions, my fishing partners got into trouble and were in need of rescue in this innocent-looking and casual section of river.

Floating lines work fine this time of year provided your egg flies are weighted, but I feel the best set-up to get your fly to the correct depth is a 2-m sink-tip. I use the Rio Versa-tip system with 1.5-m fast-sinking Airflo Polyleaders, which cast like a dream and will take your pattern to the fish.

For this system in rivers, I like to use a short 1- or 2-m tippet of 3-kg test, which allows the fly to fish at roughly the same depth as the Polyleaders.

The fishing was terrific, a perfect ending to my Stellako season as we were into many fine trout through the course of the day. It wouldn't be fair to say how many, but it was a substantial number. We caught a good assortment of sizes: a few over 50 cm, most in the 35–50-cm range, and a small portion under 35 cm.

A challenge when fishing with egg patterns is the way trout eat them, by sucking them deep into their throats, which makes hook removal difficult and can result in excessive bleeding for the trout. It's one of the reasons I shy away from fishing egg flies during mid-September, early in the sockeye run, and when there are only a few salmon in the runs. In the Stellako, I find the trout will still take dry flies until late September, so my decision was easy—fish caddis or hoppers. Very few of our Thanksgiving trout were deeply hooked, which pleased us. It was late in the season and they were more casual in their dining habits, plucking at our flies, resulting in lip hookups, which cause less stress and damage to the trout.

The Stellako egg pattern is tied exactly like the steelhead egg fly (see p. 111), but use sizes 14 and 16 Tiemco 2457 or Mustad C67S hooks and sockeye red Glo-yarn. You can also purchase single-egg beads or pre-formed yarn balls and simply bind them onto your hook.

Dragon Lake

In mid-September, Dragon Lake will have been asleep for a few months, into its summer doldrums period, the trout lying in areas of cool, oxygenated water, resting and reclusive during daylight hours. They move onto the shoals to feed only at night and in the early hours of morning when the surface temperature of the lake has been chilled by night air.

Trout sense the fast-approaching fall season, its first glimpses beginning with the frosts of September. As surface water cools, water boatmen and backswimmer flights initiate surface activity that once again kick-starts the feeding instincts of the trout, which are cruising the shoals and drop-off zones looking for the hard-shelled insects, literally chasing them all over the lake. It's an awakening signal, when the trout once again become happy

Brian Smith with a big rainbow: fall fishing at Dragon Lake.
Dale Freschi photo.

and active and the fly fisher can look forward to the heavy feeding period of fall fishing until freeze-up once again takes our sport from us.

I happily fish my rivers and the ocean from mid-July until late September while the trout lakes rest, but once fall weather cools the lakes I come back to search for the big trout of fall, eagerly anticipating a few 5-kg fish on light tackle. Other than the months of May and June on trout lakes, October is the month that will offer the largest fish of your season. In the Central Interior, Dragon Lake in Quesnel is my first choice, offering the best chance for the lunkers we search for.

The annual water boatman and ant flights, as well as sporadic late-season chironomid hatches are all that's left for surface action on lakes during early October. Water boatman activities will usually last two to three weeks, from mid-September to early October; ants will be flying sometime during the same period and chironomids will continue hatching randomly until freeze-up occurs. Most of your fishing will be with sinking lines, or floating lines and long fluorocarbon leaders when fishing shallow zones, working your flies slowly through the water column. The lake will be well oxygenated throughout; trout will be dispersed at all depths, their feeding instincts honed onto the key insects available.

Your best patterns during periods of low surface activity will be the basics of the lake smorgasbord: scuds (see p. 85), leeches (see p. 86), dragonfly nymphs (see p. 100), damselfly nymphs (see p. 99) and blood-worms (see p. 88). During late fall season, all of the above insects will begin to migrate from the shallows to deeper water for overwintering, and for a fly fisher to come across a major mass migration of any kind is like winning the lottery. If you are lucky enough to be there at the right time, recognize the happening and have the correct fly pattern, you will be blessed with a banner day. This good timing may only occur a few times in your fishing career, but will be remembered for all of your life—trust me on that.

Dragon can be a temperamental lake. Most "big fish" lakes are like that. They come on for a few short bursts each day, and leave you casting for the rest of the day. Every once in a while, during favourable solunar periods, a rising barometer and the good fortune that it's your day off, Dragon will literally kick ass and you'll clobber forty trout with 80 percent of them over 50 cm. My friend Kevin Crawford, who lives on the lake, has many of these days. He watches the lake constantly, studies and follows the solunar tables religiously, and simply looks out his window for moving fish and favour-able conditions. He'll fish those two hours of prime trout activity, release a mess of trout, and be home having a coffee by the time we can drive down there to fish the lake, and of course it's over by then.

The last burst of great fall fishing in our Interior lakes is very depen-dent upon water temperature. After the water boatman flight and the migrations of shoal-dwelling insects has petered out, there is a one- or two-week period before freeze-up when the lake will be well oxygenated, the water temperature will be between 4°C and 10°C and the trout will be ravenous—if you are lucky enough to catch it, you'll think you've died and gone to fishing heaven.

October 15 was our last kick at Dragon in 2011. Some years we can fish Dragon until the second week of November. For example, in the fall of 2008 we did very well on huge fish; our last outing was November 15. Other years, like 2011, the lake was glazed with ice by the end of October, and we missed the one week of glory before freeze-up. Dale and I did, however, catch a few hogs on our last day, the largest over 60 cm.

We had a good year.

Thoughts on Closing

Curiosity

What is it about the roughneck fishing shows on TV these days, where you have to be a young guy with a ball cap on backwards and tangle with some monster fish that has 6-inch-long teeth? Fishing, in my mind, is about the gentle side of life, where the exercise of getting there by travelling down some lonesome, dusty and muddy logging roads with a good buddy of like mind is not only part of the experience, but more often than not the best measure of your fishing day. It's also not about the size of fish you catch or don't catch, but about the scenery, the wildlife along the highway, the creeks and streams you poke your nose into along the way and sometimes about the depth of the mudholes you encounter.

Have you ever noticed that some people (like me) have a rubber neck for every piece of water they see, no matter how insignificant it is, as they truck on down the highway? It's a gift of my curious and adventurous nature when I'm in the outdoors, always wondering what's on the other side of the road and how it got there. I'm glad I still have it after all these years, that inquisitive side of my fishing personality. I think it helps me tie and design better flies, write better stories and do some thinking outside the box.

"Originators" of Fly Patterns

Well, I took a little flak from some friends and also some people I don't know when I wrote my first book, *Fly Fishing BC's Interior*. They took exception with me for naming myself an "originator" of some fly patterns in the book. Let me share some thoughts about this statement, which I have tried to express in many of my musings when it comes to original thoughts on fly patterns.

I don't think there is much original thought left in designing fly patterns, only ideas, experiments and improvements to existing models. Most fly tiers are tinkerers; we get our jollies by fiddling around with fly patterns, using materials that will adjust light, colour, movement, silhouette and the appearance of an insect we are trying to imitate. A tier looks at an "original" fly pattern and says, "Yes, but this or that material will give it the added flash, glitter, colour, feature or look that will enhance it even further." So he/she tries it and it works, slays fish by the thousands, and becomes known far and wide. The inventor/originator's name gets placed on it and he/she becomes famous for originating a fly pattern.

A good example is "my" Mikulak Sedge compared to the "original" by Art Mikulak of Calgary, Alberta. The appearance of the dressed flies is somewhat similar, but Art and I use different materials. Art used elk hair; I use deer because I feel the darker silhouette of deer hair is a better imitation of the natural caddis insect. Art staggered his clumps of wings, layering them half over the former wing, leaving noticeable gaps between them; I layer mine evenly to form a complete gap-free silhouette that appears to be one body and wing. Art's dominant body colour for his pattern was olive green; mine is a soft grey Hareline HET 2 Dark Hare's Ear, which is our principal traveller sedge colour in the Cariboo/Central Interior. Art used no hackle for his collar, or clipped it short to the shank; I use a full collar hackle, four turns each of brown and grizzly to force my pattern to ride high in the surface film. Art used a clump of clipped deer hair at the eye; I don't. These are a lot of differences. I've caught hundreds of trout on mine, and I've never seen anyone's Mikulak that looks like mine, unless it's a friend who has copied me. Am I an originator? Perhaps, but I still call mine a Mikulak, because Art gave me the first thought that got me tinkering.

The "Writing Itch"

I became a fishing writer out of curiosity. Similar to my tackling of fly fishing after I survived my teens, well after I began my fishing hobby with worms and bait (mostly because they were free and I grew up a farm boy), my writing began innocently enough as a diversion when I was stuck in Alberta for a few years with nowhere to fish for trout. I reasoned that if I couldn't feed my fishing passion with more than a few BC trips a year, I'd keep myself sane by at least writing about fishing. I wrote an article about my memories of old friend and fly-fishing mentor, Jack Shaw, who passed on in February 2000, and submitted it to Chris Marshall, editor of *Canadian Fly Fisher* magazine. I wanted to share Jack with a national magazine, as he deserved Canadian recognition and no one had really given him a last hurrah in print form. Chris kindly published my article; I gathered a little notoriety in the fly-fishing fraternity, and proceeded to scratch my writing itch a little at a time. Moving back to the BC Interior was the final motivator, as I was back in trout-fishing heaven.

I owe a great deal of my writing success to Ralph Shaw, a dear friend who lives in Courtenay and whom I don't see often enough. Ralph and Jack Shaw were not related, but were like brothers for most of their lives, living in Kamloops, fly fishing together during the heydays of the 1950s, '60s and '70s. Ralph didn't teach me to write, although he is a well-known author in his own right, but introduced me to Bob Jones, a freelance writer and former editor of *BC Outdoors* magazine. Bob took me under his wing, used his chainsaw on my first pieces of work, and cut me badly so many times I had to improve or be forever embarrassed to submit my work. Bob, however, did see some talent in me, offered encouragement with every lashing he gave, and pestered me to persevere. Bob passed on in 2008, before my first book was printed, and I often ponder what he is thinking or if he is watching me from up there... I sent him the first copy.

Dave Hughes is another author who gave me the encouragement to put four years of my life aside to write my first book. Dave has written many fine books, journals and articles on the sport. While he was editor of the *Fly Fishing and Tying Journal*, he accepted and published many of my first fly-tying articles on patterns that I had spent many years tweaking and developing. By working with Dave for a few years, even though he may not realize this, he instilled a persistent confidence in me that I carried forward to my journal writing.

Bob Graham, a trusted friend and retired engineer living in Prince George, is now my writing mentor. Bob's skill with the mechanics of the English language is now my "rock" when I write, and I value his opinions and editing skill immensely. This book is the second of mine that he has edited, and when I'm in a writing funk, he reminds me to "Stay with it, just keep musing; toss it on paper and we'll deal with it when the time comes."

Every aspiring writer needs people to knock things around with—Ralph Shaw, Bob Jones, Dave Hughes and Bob Graham were my kind of people when I needed them.

The "Fishing Thing"

It has been said, "Time waits for no man." These few years past, as I cruise through my mid-sixties, lingering thoughts about mortality stick in my head as another winter approaches: "Will these be my last days of fishing? Are there trout streams up there? Will I be invited to fish them, or will I be scorned? Is there room for yet another fly fisher and writer?" All legitimate musings I suppose, but fishing is what I like to do with my spare time during open-water season. Writing about fishing, designing and tying flies and rod-building are my choices when winter sets in. People close to me say I do too much of all of them, but I've always had trouble getting into *a little bit* of something; it has to be with both feet, or not at all. In my youth and adulthood before the age of forty, my passion was baseball and fastball, and I played with and against many of the world's best players. When I left the game in my late thirties, I never returned or played slo-pitch with the "old" boys—my run was over.

You have to put your head down and stick it out, this "fishing thing" that you have somehow managed to get into your blood. If you deny it, it can eat at you in other ways; for example, being miserable around people you love. If you embrace it, however, the relationship between you and fishing can become symbiotic. It will make you an overall happier and healthier person. The most difficult part for me is finding a balance between time for family, work, fishing and my writing itch. It's never perfect harmony, but it's the best I can do, for I'm not willing to give up on any of them to gain one over the other.

I fish because I am passionate about it. For example, compare playing golf to fly fishing. They are similar but the differences are intriguing: good exercise in beautiful places (one manicured, one not), fine company (if you choose your partner wisely), expensive equipment (or not) and good and bad days (especially with golf). I do both, but my fishing appetite trumps golf, which is why I will probably never get my handicap lower than 24 because I'm usually fishing instead of golfing. Besides, I can't afford to play golf as much as I fish. I suppose, however, if you worked the costs out, the price of a yearly golf membership versus a life of fishing would likely be a wash once you consider the cost of everything you need to be keen at either one: clubs, carts, bags, balls for golf; rods, boats, tackle and gizmos for fishing. On the flip side of the coin, I don't think golfers or fly fishers are ever completely happy with their equipment or tackle, always looking for a new "feel" in your ball or club, or "tweak" to your tackle or rods that will hopefully offer you an advantage in your sport. I've come to the conclusion that no matter what becomes your passion outside of family life, it's going to cost a bunch of time and money to do it, so you may as well enjoy it to the best of your ability.

If I've learned anything about my sport, it's that fishing can take you to places that are wild, free and uncluttered, optimistically with companions of a common mind. It can be a constant resource to enrich your soul and help you appreciate things that are "no charge" except for the gasoline to get there, a few of your own hand-tied flies and perhaps a few metres of tippet material. For me, fishing has been a lifetime of challenges and thoughts, some deeper than others, but mostly just plain fun with people in surroundings that I enjoy immensely. I just hope that place up yonder has a trout stream for me to play in.

Appendix: *Camping Spots*

Central Interior Camping

When friends come to fish your home waters, you want them to catch a few trout, have a quality camping experience and take a few memories home with them. If a fly fisher is looking to stay at a fishing resort, there is a limited supply of them on Central Interior lakes and rivers, which is not a totally bad thing, but it restricts fly fishers' opportunities unless they are willing to set up base camp at the resorts, fish home water during the evening and drive out to explore other waters during the day.

Many lakes and rivers have Forest Service sites that offer unsurpassed wilderness camping, but you need to be self-contained, put up with a few persistent bugs in the backcountry, and be willing to "rough it" a little. The no-charge campsites are user-maintained with pit toilets, fire pits and rough boat launches, and are generally clean and well looked after by Forest Service contractors.

The Central Interior is bear country—both grizzly and black—but if you keep your camp clean and tidy, the bears are not considered to be pests and there are few encounters. For the most part, they prefer to be left alone and will vacate the area when humans are around. However, the usual precautions are in order when camping in bear country: carry a whistle and use it to make noise when walking wilderness trails; have bear spray available; and keep small children under surveillance at all times.

Prince George North

If you want some amenities, Vivian Lake is a great little place to set up camp. It's close to the city, offers cabins and campsites, and is central enough to be within an hour's drive of some of the best fishing north of Prince George. Vivian is also a quality fishing lake on its own merits, stocked annually by the provincial Freshwater Fisheries Society with up to twenty thousand brook and rainbow trout. From Vivian, you can easily hike into the lakes of Eskers Park, walk down the road with your belly boat and fish Verdant Lake or drive north of the city to fish lakes within an hour of the city: Hart, Boundary, Freya, Eena or the Crooked River system.

Farther north on Hwy 97, about a forty-minute drive from Prince George, is a marvellous provincial campsite called Crooked River Provincial Park, which offers the best family-oriented camping in the area. Situated on little Bear Lake, which has an excellent swimming beach, the campsite allows access to a number of lakes in the vicinity. Square Lake is a twenty-minute hike with a float tube; Hart Lake, for boat fishing, is a ten-minute hike or short drive down the paved highway; Wicheeda, Crystal, Emerald and Tacheeda lakes are all within a twenty-minute to one-hour drive. Or, fish the Crooked River system, which can be a twenty-minute hike from the campsite into Livingstone Springs, or a short drive along the 200 Road or 100 Road to access the river's rich fishing waters.

Even farther north along Hwy 97, about a ninety-minute drive from Prince George, camping is available at two more provincial parks. One is Whiskers Point on McLeod Lake, and the other, a further fifteen minutes up the highway, is Tudyah Lake. Whiskers is more developed than Tudyah, has a better swimming beach and boat launch, but both provide access to more excellent fishing waters such as Firth, Junkers, Bruce and Trappers lakes, and the McLeod, Misinchinka, Parsnip and Pine rivers and their tributaries. You begin to enter grayling country as you explore the

Parsnip River system and streams north of it, so be prepared to fish dry flies for these stunning northern beauties.

A fly fisher will not be forgiven if he or she doesn't take the half-hour drive to cross Pine Pass and try the Pine River, an absolutely gorgeous little stream that skirts Hwy 97 through the pass to Chetwynd. As you cross and drop over the pass, the Pine is a small river accessible from logging roads at its headwaters from Azouzetta Lake below the Pine Pass summit, or from numerous pullouts along the highway. As you will find with most rivers along the highway, be prepared to walk a couple of corners up or down the river to access better fishing places.

Southwest of Fort McLeod, Carp Lake Provincial Park beckons the fly fisher to a remote setting within an area steeped in early Carrier First Nations history. From this campsite, you can either fish big Carp Lake by boat or backpack into numerous lakes and rivers in the surrounding area. This is a magnificent spot in northern BC's wilderness. Try the hiking trail along the McLeod River from where it exits Carp Lake, or venture west along the Tsiloch and Davie Muskeg Forest Service roads to greet the headwaters of the McLeod before it enters the great lake.

Prince George West

Fly fishers working Hwy 16 west of Prince George are limited to motels or Forest Service campsites until 130 km west at Fort Fraser, where Beaumont Provincial Park is situated at the east end of Fraser Lake. This is a great spot, a place where Lois and I have enjoyed many wonderful memories of when our girls were small. The park has everything your family could wish for: a great swimming beach for kids, hiking trails, an upscale boat launch suitable for ski boats, sanitation dump, flush toilets and close access to supplies at Fort Fraser. This campsite is the location of the original Fort Fraser, established in 1806 by Simon Fraser as a fur-trading post, which was fully operational until 1915. Remnants of fort buildings still remain—it's a place to pay homage to the explorers who forged this province.

From Beaumont, there are many day-trip spots to fish within a one-hour drive, including the Stellako River about thirty minutes west of the campsite. However, if fly fishing were my only goal, I would choose Stellako

Lodge or Nithi on the Lake campsites as headquarters. Stellako Lodge sits on the river mouth exiting from Francois Lake; Nithi is on Francois Lake about five minutes from the Glenannan Bridge.

You can fish the Stellako during its best times—early morning and late evening—and make day runs to the productive lakes and streams south of Francois Lake, such as Anzus, Borel, Graham, Trout, Binta, Uncha and Takysie lakes, and all of the walk-in waters of the area. Each of these spots has FS campsites that are rarely full during open-water season; many are unoccupied when I visit them. Uncha and Takysie have resort operations as well as FS campsites.

A venture north of Vanderhoof up Hwy 27 to Fort St. James opens up a realm of fishing opportunities that I have yet to explore, country that could fill a book on its own merits—a myriad of lakes, rivers and creeks, some flowing north to the Arctic through the Nation River system, and a number traversing south to Stuart Lake and the Fraser River system.

About 55 km west of Prince George, between Bednesti and Cluculz lakes, the Bobtail FS Road will strike southwest from Hwy 16 West and lead you into more good camping spots and unhurried fishing water. On the Bobtail Road, bear south at the 37-km junction where the Bobtail Tatuk Road connects, and you'll come across Eulatazella and Bobtail lakes. These lakes are not known for their fly fishing, but both have FS campsites and will provide day-trip access to Grizzly West and Woodcock lakes and everything surrounding them. Grizzly West also has a good FS recreation site, suitable for car-top boat launching.

On Hwy 16 West about 65 km west of Prince George, Finnmore Road cuts north toward the Nechako River, and at about the 6-km mark, a marked gravel road will lead you on a short track to Cobb Lake, which has an excellent FS campsite for four to six units, boat launch and pit toilets. The road access is suitable for all sizes of RV rigs. Cobb gets busy on weekends, but is pretty quiet during the week, and is well suited to family camping trips.

Vanderhoof South

From the village of Vanderhoof, the Kenney Dam Road swings south and meanders southwest 90 km to Kenney Dam on Knewstubb Lake, where the once free-flowing Nechako River was dammed in the 1950s to form the

Nechako Reservoir, which provides power to the Alcan smelter at Kitimat through the Kemano powerhouse.

Along the route and close to Vanderhoof are Nulki and Tachik lakes, which have resort fishing camps and provide good family accommodation. Farther along, there is excellent resort accommodation at Nechako Lodge on Knewstubb Lake, but that's it for the Kenney Dam Road except for FS campsites on the Nechako River.

At a junction on the Kenney Dam Road, you can travel directly south on the Kluskus FSR, which accesses more wilderness accommodations and resort camping facilities at Tatuk and Finger lakes. For fly-fishing people, these resorts can offer fly-in or horseback trail opportunities as well as local information as to where the trout are biting for your day trips to remote waters of the area.

If you wish to be more secluded at a FS recreation site, Hobson Lake off the Kluskus west on the 500 Road is a central spot that offers trophy trout when they are on. For a day trip, a one-hour hike from Hobson Lake campsite into Chief Gray Lake will uncover a stocked wilderness lake where you can tackle trout up to 3 kg.

Prince George South and West Road (Blackwater) River Country

The Blackwater Road, which heads south of Prince George off Hwy 16 West within city limits, offers fly fishers a host of camping and fishing opportunities. Again, you won't find resorts to pamper you, but if you like to camp you will always be able to find seclusion, great fly fishing and quiet places that will kindle fond memories for the remainder of your life.

West Lake Provincial Park is 14 km south on the Blackwater and offers day-use facilities but has no camping accommodations. If you're pulling a speedboat and have a carload of kids on your camping journey and need to burn off some gasoline, West Lake is your best bet along this route for the kids to let off some energy—the boat launch is the best around, and is only ten minutes from my property.

Travelling due south on the Blackwater Road, which turns to good gravel after Baldy Hughes, you'll come across FS sites at Mackenzie West and East and Punchaw lakes, again not known for great fishing. But, I urge you to drive thirty or so more kilometres down to the Blackwater Crossing FS campsite, where you'll find the best camping spot on the road. After the middle of June when the river opens (to fly fishing only) you'll be able to fish one of the most remote and beautiful rivers of the north. You'll do a lot of walking and exploring along this river, but the further you walk or drive the less the pressure and the better the fishing will be.

If you take the Pelican FSR, which swings southwest off the Blackwater Road at about the 30-km marker, good FS recreation sites are available at Tory, Barton, Lintz, Meadow, Tagai, Kevin and Pelican lakes. Lintz has the best boat launch of the bunch and is central to these waters if you wish to do a little day tripping to explore all the fishing opportunities of the Pelican FS Road.

The upper Chilako River crosses the Pelican FS Road at several spots, and can be followed to its outlet from Tatuk Lake by bearing west onto the Pelican Chilako (100) FS Road at the 49-km mark of the Pelican FS Road. The road runs about 50 km to Tatuk Lake. If you feel like scrambling through the willows to fish the Chilako, there are spots and corners on the river that will produce non-stop action for trout to 1 kg.

From Blackwater Crossing FS site, cross the river and drive another several kilometres, and you'll come to the Batnuni Road at the top of the hill. The road cuts west along the river valley crest and drops down to the Batnuni Bridge Crossing, site of another small FS campsite that will access the river above and below the bridge.

About another 6 km along the Batnuni Road, the Nazko Road bears south, takes you past Gillies Crossing and leads you to the West Road (Blackwater) River campsite at the Nazko Bridge, probably one of my favourite places in the entire world. It's not like it used to be, before the pine beetle infestation killed the mature pines that adorned the site, but it remains a beautiful river and has a revered place in my heart. I'll surely be fly fishing here when I'm gone and my ashes are spread in this quiet river of my dreams.

Further south along the Nazko Road, as it meanders through the lush valley, the village of Nazko for supplies and Marmot Lake campsite offers the fly fisher a central location to fish more enchanted waters including the productive Marmot Lake, where 2- and 3-kg trout are common quarry.

The still waters around Marmot are numerous: Fishpot, Crater, Redwater and Bishop lakes. The area's small tributaries of the Blackwater are also intriguing: Nazko, Baezaeko, Coglistiko and Snaking. The river trout are wild Blackwater strain, and while some of the lakes are stocked, many contain the wild Blackwater strain—all are rambunctious, fighting rainbows. This area is truly a fishing Mecca.

Prince George East

The rough but beautiful country nestling against the McGregor and Rocky Mountains east of Prince George is another area with an abundance of fly-fishing water that sees few visitors through an angling season. It's quite desolate with very few supply and service depots, so for camping it's important to have a vehicle that's in good repair, and enough gasoline and supplies to last your vacation. Once you are in this wilderness, you could be several hours' drive to the nearest store or village to replenish provisions.

Travelling east from Prince George on Hwy 16, a short drive of forty minutes brings you to Purden Lake Provincial Park, which is the area's best bet for organized family camping that offers a good ski boat launch, beach swimming in a clean, clear lake and treed sites in a gorgeous forested setting of white and blue spruce and firs. Fly fishing is okay at Purden, but you won't enjoy competing with recreational boats. Purden will, however, work as a headquarters to access remote waters and hiking trails south and west of your campsite.

South of Purden there are some Forest Service and many rough recreation sites on lakes that are seldom fished and rivers that beckon the fly fisher to visit. Before Purden, the Willow North FS Road runs due south along the Willow River, which has FS Rec Sites near the Hwy 16 junction and farther along about 15 km at Willow Bend, where there is a junction and the Willow FSR South continues on through logging roads to the river's headwaters near Wells and Barkerville.

South of Prince George about 15 km, the Willow FS (1000) Road breaks due east off Hwy 97 North and will also lead you to the Willow Bend Rec Site. Along this route, there are many lakes with FS Rec Sites: Francis and Ste. Marie along the road, or Opatcho, Wansa, Ispah, Pitoney and Grizzly

Lake East's FS sites gained by short access roads, where you can set camp and fish to your heart's content in secluded wilderness settings.

The Beaver Bowron FSR cuts southeast of Hwy 16 East just before Purden Lake Provincial Park, joining the Bowron FSR about 18 km east. The Bowron FSR runs south along the Bowron River to access many isolated lakes and streams, all of them containing wild and coarse fish—rainbows, Dolly Vardens, pike minnows and whitefish. There are no established FS campsites along this route, but many rough camping areas at various lakes that are suitable for self-contained units—Tumuch, Pinkerton and Papoose lakes. It's rough, but the pristine beauty of this area is incredible.

On the north side of Hwy 16 East, just past the Purden Lake park, you can take the Bowron FSR, cross the Fraser River between the logging communities of Hansard and McGregor, and follow the Rocky Mountain Trench along the Rocky Mountain Highway. Or take the Pass Lake or Church FS roads to access the spectacular wilderness north of the Fraser River. There are established FS campsites at Pass and Amanita lakes, where you can fish or journey to some wild, amazing free-flowing rivers that course from the Rockies to the Fraser River—the McGregor, Torpy and Herrick rivers and their tributaries. Or wander over to the Arctic and Pacific divide area of the trench, and fish the Parsnip and its tributaries: the Anzac, Hominka, Missinka, Table and Misinchinka rivers. This is grayling, Dolly Varden and bull trout country, isolated and rough, but a place where you can explore freely and without the pressure of other anglers.

The weather on this side of the Fraser can be unpredictable. Storms can gather in minutes, you can be rained or hailed upon without warning, and you need to be sheltered and prepared to ride out all measure of conditions for short periods of time. July and early August will offer the camper the most favourable weather.

Quesnel and North Cariboo

If you're on your way south during the months of May and June or September and October, you should stop overnight at Dragon Lake, where you may end up staying if the fishing is on. There is no better chance of tangling with a 5-kg trout than at Dragon Lake, where the rich nutrients of the big lake's waters grow trout that pack on 1 kg per year, and will greedily consume your flies if they are in the right mood.

Because it's shallow and weedy, Dragon warms up too much in the summer months and the trout get sulky, but during spring and fall when the water is cooler they key on the hatches of mayflies, chironomids, damsels, caddis and boatmen, and always on the ever-present scuds, leeches and dragonflies that form their diet.

There are three campsites on Dragon Lake: Robert's Roost and Legion Beach on the north end, and a private campsite on the south end operated by Abb and Linda. The "Roost" is accessed by Gook Road, the other two by Dragon Lake Road. It's city camping, but a great place to take a break and perhaps take a trophy trout.

Ten Mile Lake Provincial Park, a few kilometres north of Quesnel, is another spot that can be useful if you have children in tow. They will love the beach, trails and amenities, welcoming a break from highway boredom.

A visit to Barkerville along Hwy 26 East makes for an interesting side journey if you have the time and wish to show the family a little Canadian history by resting at one of the many campsites in this historic area. During the gold rush of the mid-1800s, Barkerville was the largest city (town) west of Chicago!

I've touched on some of the accessible places to pitch your camp in the Central Interior. Within 200 km of the hub city of Prince George, there are several hundred lakes, rivers and streams that have rainbow trout inventory. Many have small FS campsites, lots of firewood and are uncrowded— lots of room to enjoy northern hospitality, wilderness style. Happy fishing!

Index

BRIAN SMITH is a fly fisher, freelance outdoor writer and photographer. He was a recipient of the 2008 BC Federation of Fly Fishers Jack Shaw Fly Tying Award for his creative fly-tying art. Over the past decade, his writing has been featured in many journals and magazines, including the *Prince George Citizen*, *Fly Fishing and Tying Journal*, *The Art of BC Fly Fishing 2005* Calendar, *The Canadian Fly Fisher* magazine and *BCWF Outdoor Edge* magazine. Smith has fly fished BC's waters for over forty-five years, has four adult children and lives with his wife Lois in Prince George, BC. *Seasons of a Fly Fisher* is his second book; his first book, *Fly Fishing BC's Interior*, was published by Caitlin Press in 2009.

Caitlin Press Inc.
8100 Alderwood Road | Halfmoon Bay, BC | VON IYI
www.caitlin-press.com

Text design by Kathleen Fraser.
Cover design by Vici Johnstone.
· Edited by Patricia Wolfe.
Fly photos and preliminary editing by Bob Graham.
Printed in Canada.

Caitlin Press Inc. acknowledges financial support from the Government of Canada through the Canada Book Fund and the Canada Council for the Arts, and from the Province of British Columbia through the British Columbia Arts Council and the Book Publisher's Tax Credit.

Canada Council   Conseil des arts
for the Arts   du Canada

BRITISH COLUMBIA
ARTS COUNCIL
An agency of the Province of British Columbia

Library and Archives Canada Cataloguing in Publication

Smith, Brian, 1947-
    Seasons of a fly fisher : fly fishing Canada's western
waters / Brian Ivan Smith.

Includes index.
ISBN 978-1-927575-05-5

    1. Fly fishing—British Columbia. 2. Fly fishing—
Alberta. 3. Flies, Artificial. 4. Fly tying. I. Title.

SH572.B8S655 2013   799.12'409711   C2013-900532-3